LIFE EVOLUTION

37 Ways to Transform Your Life

Graham Nicholls

ABOUT THE AUTHOR

H ey there!

Please allow me to introduce myself, my name is Graham Nicholls and first up I'd like to offer my sincerest gratitude to you for choosing my book. I can't accurately express in words how thankful I am that I am able to offer my thoughts to you through my writing.

For over twenty years now I have been helping people to change and improve their lives and all whilst going on a journey of my own. My story into the world of personal change starts in my kitchen and is a day I will never forget.

It was a sunny Sunday afternoon, late on in summer and I had just gotten home after working all day. It was nice and warm outside, I could hear kids playing somewhere off in the distance with a dog barking and the smell of a barbeque was drifting on the slight breeze.

However, I was in no mood to enjoy the fruits of summer as I was feeling as low as I'd ever felt. I was standing hunched over the counter top, only just holding myself up with my arms and with my head hung downwards. I was jolted out of my state by a voice from the doorway behind me, "Are you ok Graham?"

I jumped a bit as I spun around to see my parents stood at the door, my mum had a concerned look on her face seeing me stood there like that. I did what I had always done and picked myself up, put a smile on my face and replied by saying that yes I was fine, just tired from a long day at work.

The truth is that I had been doing that for quite some time, pretending to everyone else that everything was fine and that I was ok. To everyone else I was this laid back person who didn't let the world bother him and who would always do anything to help everyone. Inside me, however, there was turmoil!

I invited my parents in and told them to go and sit down while I fixed some drinks and, as with everyone else, they accepted my explanation and did as I suggested. I had become pretty good at the lies and fooling everyone! In the next moment everything was about to change and the journey was about to start.

As I reached up into the cupboard to get out some glasses for the drinks I was fixing my parents one of them slipped from my grip. I grasped at air but could do nothing more than watch in slow motion as the glass tumbled and fell. It bounced off my arm and headed towards to counter top and then it bounced off of that as well, heading towards its final destination.

As the glass smashed on the floor I felt everything drain away from me and my legs gave way. As my parents rushed back into the kitchen they found me sat down on the floor, my head in my hands and sobbing uncontrollably.

The following morning I found myself in a doctor's office, I didn't really know how I had gotten there but in front of me was a doctor telling me that I was suffering from Depression, Anxiety and Stress. I sat there dumbfounded, how had I got to this place in my life? What on earth was going on? Depression? Anxiety? Stress? That couldn't be right, I was the most laid back man in the world...... wasn't I?

I walked out of the doctors with a slip of paper in my hand, a pre-scription for some medication to "help me out" - at least that's what the doctor said. The only problem being that the medication wouldn't start working for around three months and I didn't want to wait that long to start feeling better.

In that moment I decided not to fulfil that prescription and find out as much as I could about Depression, Anxiety and Stress. That moment changed my life and for the last twenty-plus years I've studied how to help myself and others and it has brought me to this point and this book.

In this book you'll discover the top thirty seven tips to evolve your life into the one you want, so how about we get started. You don't need to use all thirty seven, all I suggest to you is that you go through each of them and pick the ones that resonate with you, the ones that you see working for you, the ones that sound right.

At this point I can only hope that you enjoy the book....... On to point number one!

EVOLUTION POINT NUMBER ONE

Take Responsibility

"The final forming of a person's character lies in their own hands"

- *Anne Frank*

T ake Responsibility

It wasn't until I took responsibility for my life that I started to truly recover and break free of the chains of Depression, Anxiety and Stress. In fact, I would go so far as to say that not taking responsibility for my life was one of the major reasons for me feeling those emotions in the first place.

"Are you saying that everything that has happened to me in the past is my responsibility Graham?" - this is a very common question I get asked by coaching clients, and one you might be asking having read that first paragraph. No, that's not what I am saying. Our lives involve other people and other circumstances that will not always work to our advantage, these are things we can never be in control of. However, you should take responsibility for how you act and react in every situation.

The problem is that in many countries around the world there has developed a "take them to court" culture in which we sue everyone for anything. This removes the very essence of responsibility as the cry of "it wasn't my fault" is heard ringing from every side of the globe.

Let me give you a typical example:

You can imagine that you are driving along a straight road, it's a nice day and you can see clearly in front of you. There are no cars ahead of you so you have the road to yourself. As you approach a side road you see another car pull up to the junction but you have the right of way so you carry on. All of a sudden this car pulls out in front of you having not seen you coming and WHACK...... you crash into the side of him.

What level of responsibility do you hold in this instance?

Thanks to the 'take them to court' culture there will be many people that shout "NONE, I HOLD NO RESPONSIBILITY, IT'S THEIR FAULT" - However, someone who has taken responsibility for their life may just have a different answer, let's go and revisit the situation.

Imagine again that you are driving along that same road, it's still a nice day and there is nothing in front of you so you have the road to yourself. As you approach that same side road you see a car pull up to the junction. Despite the fact that you have the right of way you consider the possibility that he doesn't see you and therefore keep a close eye on him as you approach. All of a sudden he pulls out in front of you...... but you've seen it coming, you took responsibility for being prepared so you are able to react, brake, swerve and avoid the accident.

Just imagine if you were to do that in every area of your life; take responsibility to see what is ahead of you, be prepared for it and then take the correct actions when it arrived. What would happen to your life if, from this moment on, you started to do just that? Would you avoid some collisions in the future (and I'm not just talking on the roads here!)?

Of course, some things do happen that we simply cannot avoid so how can we possibly take responsibility for them? The truth is we cannot always take responsibility for what happens....... BUT .... We can take responsibility for our actions and reactions to every situation we face.

The 'actions' that I refer to above are the behaviours we exhibit every day and taking control of those behaviours means you are taking responsibility for them. In every situation we have a choice of how to behave, how to act. When things go well we can act by jumping up and down, waving our arms in the air, having a party or many other ways, but it is generally when things don't go well that our choices are challenged.

Our behaviours are usually driven by our reactions and those reactions are our emotions. Our emotional system reacts much quicker than our behavioural system and, if let loose, can be the cause of our poor, negative behaviours. It is the moment between reaction and action that our responsibility sits, it is in that moment that we have a choice that can drastically change the course of that experience, that day or even our lives.

Let's go back and look at the example from earlier:

You've just narrowly missed the car that pulled out on you and you have slammed on your breaks and screeched to a halt..... What is next? The person in the other car has made a mistake and nearly caused an accident that could have injured you both, or worse. What is your reaction and action?

Let's say that you react with anger, the red mist descends and fury takes over. You open your door, get out and storm over to the other car ready to drag the driver from their seat and set about them either verbally, or worse, physically. Have you heard of cases of road rage where both parties lives were changed forever? So you get to the car and fling open the door...... but you find a little old lady inside crying, it turns out that she's just had a call to say her husband has had a heart attack and she's panicking, all she wanted to do was get to the hospital as quickly as possible and she didn't see you coming.

Rewind a little...... imagine now that you react with anger but as the red mist starts to descend you take responsibility for your actions and reactions so you stop the emotional and behavioural response. You realise that you have no idea who the other person is let alone what is happening in their life so you decide to react in a better way and go to see if they are ok.

Responsibility or no responsibility? That is the question!

To quote a Bon Jovi song:

Welcome to wherever you are,
This is your life and you've made it this far.
Welcome, you've got to believe,
Right here right now you're exactly where you are supposed to be.

In every moment of your life you have a choice, a choice of how to react and act and that in itself holds great responsibility. However, as George Zaluki said:

"Responsibility, surely, is nothing more than the ability to respond"

Each and every one of us has the ability to respond, it is the activation of that ability for the benefit of ourselves and others that really matters. When is now a good time to take responsibility for and within your life? (read that again!)

Take Responsibility!

EVOLUTION POINT NUMBER TWO

Develop a Morning Routine

"Your morning routine generates a 10 times return for either good or for bad - make it good!"

- *Todd Stocker*

Develop a Morning Routine

Have I convinced you to take responsibility for your life, actions and reactions? The truth is that some people will have read that first chapter and then closed the book. You are still here so I've got a good idea that you really are ready to keep evolving your life.

There are so many quotes about mornings and morning routines that it was particularly hard to choose one for this chapter. I wanted something that had not been over used such as, "if you win the first hour of the day, you win the entire day" - I'm sure you have heard that before.

I'm not here to tell you what your morning routine should be, that is you responsibility. I do, however, want to encourage you to set a morning routine that benefits you so I'm going to give you some ideas of what you might want to consider including.

I used to be the person who hit the snooze button and head off back to sleep. In fact, in my younger years I would purposefully set my alarm 30 minutes early knowing that I could hit the snooze button 3 times and get up on the fourth sounding of the alarm.

There has been much research done into what happens to our body when we hit that snooze button and go back to sleep. When we do this we effectively go back into a sleep cycle and the average human being sleeps in cycles of around 90 minutes. Hitting the snooze button and being woken after just nine or ten minutes means that you body is still within that sleep cycle...... is it any wonder I was so tired all the time!

Now, I know I said earlier that I wasn't going to tell you what your morning routine should be. Hopefully, however, you will have clicked onto the fact that the snooze button is simply not your friend. Without a doubt, your best course of action is to get up the moment your alarm goes off and get yourself moving. I once heard someone say, during a speech they were giving, that they aim to have their feet on the floor within thirty seconds of their alarm going off....... I've stuck to that ever since.

Start the hydration process early. We all know how important it is to stay hydrated and getting that process started first thing in the morning helps your system to start up. Whether you have a glass of water waiting by your bed that you can swig down, or you grab one from the tap straight away.... Start the hydration process.

We were born and made to move, that's what the human body is for and getting that process started as early in the day as possible also set you up for the day. While we move a little in our sleep, it is not enough to keep our system going. In fact, sleep is about shutting our system down for a rest isn't it. So we need to wake our entire system up.

Movement is the only way to do that so consider how you are going to move first thing in the morning, and I'm not talking about just moving your arm up and down and side to side while you brush your teeth. Whether it's a walk, jog, run, cycle or visit to the gym you need to get that body of yours moving. It helps with blood flow, it helps with waste flow and it helps with energy flow so you need to get into your flow.

Consider for a moment, what will you do to move your body first thing in the morning?

The next couple of suggestions I have for you are covered in much greater detail later in the book so I'll be brief with them. First up is gratitude! As we rise in the morning we have a choice, right there and then, of how we want to act throughout the day. What mood do we want to start the day in? Do you know anyone who is 'always grumpy' in the morning? I know I've met some people like that. I've also met people who can't possibly speak and be nice until they have had their first cup of coffee!

Choosing gratitude first thing in the morning puts you into an amazing frame of mind and selects the attitude early on. Taking the time to consider just three things you are grateful for and focus on them for a short period, it is such an empowering way to start each day. You could even incorporate this into the movement part of the routine and double up your effectiveness.

My next suggestion is Meditation; again, it will be covered in more detail later in the book. You can incorporate gratitude into your meditation practice as well and double its effectiveness. I really do struggle to explain just how powerful meditation in the morning is to me and my day. That time to just let everything go and be free in my mind, to breathe in and out thoroughly and be at peace with me is incredible.

Finally, of course, we need to talk about what not to do or at least my suggestions of what not to do. I have just one of these and it's the one that gets talked a fair amount these days. Stay off any type of phone, tablet, laptop, PC etc etc etc. Let them be for a while and just be with yourself and your routine, focus on that. Feeding your brain with loads of digitised information first thing in the morning just doesn't feel right to me. That first forty five minutes to an hour are when our brain needs space to wake up, reboot itself and come alive. You have the rest of the day to kill it with info, give it a chance to live first!

There are no big secrets to a morning routine, it should be simple yet effective so I heartily recommend that you consider what your morning routine will be and stick to it.

Feeling alive first thing in the morning leaves you alive for the rest of the day!

What will your morning routine be from this moment on?

Develop a Morning Routine!

EVOLUTION POINT NUMBER THREE

Foster Gratitude

"Gratitude makes sense of the past, brings peace for today, and creates a vision for tomorrow"

- *Melody Beattie*

Foster Gratitude

The power of gratitude is immeasurable and unimaginable, it finds a way to brush virtually anything aside and stands tall in your life no matter the circumstance. It is like Superman's strength or Spiderman's ability to climb walls, it is your superpower and you can turn it on within a moment.

Some years ago it was discovered that the human brain has a 'gate system' when it comes to feeling emotions in which one emotion can close the gate on another and take over. Have you ever been in a really happy place and something happened that almost instantly made you sad, angry or frustrated. Those emotions firmly closed the gate on your happiness and they did it without saying please or thank you for letting them in.

Gratitude has the power to close the gate on any negative emotion...... then lock the gate so that they can't get back in for a while. The best part about gratitude is that the shift to it is nothing more than a thought away. A simple thought of something or someone you are grateful for can shift you away from any negative feelings and into a more positive and productive state. Let's try it shall we?

Take the time, just for a few quick moments to answer the following question in your mind:

-   If you could be, what would you be grateful for right now?

Just think of one thing in your life that you could be grateful for, focus on it for a while and remember why it is you are grateful for it. You could even close your eyes and see it in bright vivid colours and as you do so you can feel the gratitude starting to fill your heart. The magical words that make gratitude stronger are ones we use every day, Thank You! Our whole system knows that when we say those two words we are giving thanks for something and our body and mind react. Say thank you for whatever it is you are focussing on...... say Thank You.

Now that you have that firmly in your mind and gratitude is filling your heart and working its way around your system, answer the following question:

-   If you could, WHO would you be grateful in your life right now?

Think of a person who is in your life, or who has been in your life at some point, that you are totally grateful for. Place your focussing completely on that person, you know what they look like, you can hear their voice, you can feel the gratitude you have for them. Be right there, in that moment right now. Tell them, in your mind, why you are so grateful for them and then use those two magical words again...... Thank you.

How do you feel right now? It's amazing just how quickly the simple act of focussing on what you can be grateful for shifts your entire system. It's amazing just how powerful the words "Thank You" are to our lives, we use them in our everyday lives and we can use them to affect our entire being.

What, therefore, is fostering gratitude? To foster gratitude, for me, means to nurture it every day and help it to grow into your life. Making gratitude one of your first thoughts and experiences of the day in the morning frees up your mind for the day ahead. Making it one of your last thoughts and experiences before sleeping gives your mind the peace it needs to rest.

You'll notice that I use experience as well as thought, why is that? You may ask. I honestly believe that gratitude is a powerful thought and an unstoppable experience and that the experience makes you unstoppable. Many people have a gratitude journal in which they write down each day what they have to be grateful for in their lives, which is a great way to start and yet this is just the 'thought' part of the process. To get the experience we need to live it in that moment.

When I asked you the question above about what you could be grateful for, I didn't just rely on the answer. I went a step further and asked you focus on what you are grateful for, focus in on it fully so that you experience it and know that gratitude is filling your heart. I also asked you to say to yourself the words "Thank You" as they heighten the experience. Saying those words out loud make that experience all the more powerful.

How to foster gratitude:

Get yourself a Gratitude Journal, it doesn't matter if it is just a notebook, a diary or a proper journal. Write down, first thing in the morning and last thing at night, 5 things / people that you are grateful for. Of those five things, make at least two of them things that you haven't mentioned before so that you are thinking of new things and people every day.

Then, take a few minutes to focus on your top two and be completely grateful for them. See them, hear them (if they make a noise) and feel the gratitude filling your heart and circulating your system. Then say Thank You for them, out loud if you can, and repeat those thanks three times for each. Completely and utterly get into the experience and let those feelings of gratefulness take over you.

Taking those five or six minutes out, twice a day, can be life changing as you are practicing and nurturing your natural gratitude state so that if and when you need it, gratefulness can show up in your life and firmly slam the gate on those emotions you do not want or need.

Foster Gratitude!

EVOLUTION POINT NUMBER FOUR

Breathe Effectively

"Breath is the bridge which connects life to conscious-ness, which unites your body to your thoughts. When-ever your mind becomes scattered, use your breath as the means to take hold of your mind again"

- *Thich Nhat Hanh*

Breathe Effectively

Breathe Effectively Have you ever considered what your body needs most, from a physical needs point of view? As human beings, we can go without food for a few weeks and we can go without water for a few days but we can only go without air for a few minutes.

I watched a documentary recently about the human system and its physical needs, how best to feed and water it. On it there was a man who was trying to break the world record for how long he could hold his breath under water, do you know how long he lasted?

I was astonished to see that he could hold his breath for 21 minutes...... yes twenty one minutes! Now, I don't recommend trying this as he had trained for a long time and had medical professionals on hand in case something went wrong. What this proves, is my point above, we need air more than anything else from a physical standpoint.

Yet, all too often, we take it for granted and just let our body get on with it, the daily motion of breathing in and out. It stands to reason though, that if we need it more than food and water then, surely, it must be a more important process than eating and drinking - something we often place great focus on!

The old saying of 'just take a deep breath' when you are upset, stressed, overwhelmed or generally out of balance could not be a greater truth if it tried. Focussing on our breath for as little as three minutes can create a massive change in both our physical and mental wellbeing. Imagine having that power at your fingertips (metaphorically speaking) and all it takes is doing something that you do all day anyway, amazing.

Breathing exercises have been part of many cultures and practices for centuries, whether it be meditation, mindfulness, yoga, tai chi or martial arts, they all utilise breathing to control emotional state. Let's take martial arts as an example; martial artists use breathing to aid focus when completing complicated routines or breaking things with bare hands or feet. In other disciplines breathing is used to clear the mind, relax the mind or to enter a particular emotional state.

Just how powerful is breathing effectively? Consider for a minute, if you will, that we now know that breathing is not only a necessity to our physical health but it is also a powerful tool to our mental and emotional health. That's power right!
It goes further than that though, it has been proven that using effective breathing can stave off illness and infection while also creating energy throughout our body. In short, breathing effectively can be linked to virtually every aspect of our wellbeing! Isn't it time you learned to breathe effectively?

It's hard for me to take you through a breathing exercise just describing them in words so I'm going to suggest that you take some time to go out and do some research for yourself. Here's a list of a few breathing techniques that you may want to look up:

- Heart Activation Breathing
- 3 Minute Breathing Space Exercise
- 4-7-8 Breathing Exercise (for stress and anxiety)
- Diaphragmatic Breathing (also known as Abdominal Breathing)
- Lions Breathe Exercise (also known as the "Ha" Breathing Exercise)
- Alternate Nostril Breathing Exercise (for focus)
- Humming Bee Breath (for calmness)
- Equal Breathing (for relaxation)
- Breath of Fire (for energy)

Or you could just go into your favourite search engine online and type in "Breathing Exercises for............ and fill in the blank.

It's over to you....... Breathe Effectively!

EVOLUTION POINT NUMBER FIVE

Leave Judgement Aside

"When you judge another you do not define them, you define yourself"

- *Anon*

L eave Judgement Aside

I once saw a quote that said something along the lines of *"to judge someone is human but to keep your thoughts to yourself is a choice"* and I remember thinking that it was a terrible thing to say! Judging someone is not being human in the slightest, judging someone is a thought and a choice and not a very nice one at that.

Should we choose to judge someone we are effectively saying that we are better than them, that we know more than them in some way, shape or form. In that moment we completely ignore the fact that they have a life that we know nothing about. Even if it is someone we know, we still cannot possible conceive of all the aspects of their life, both externally and internally.

The moment a judgement is made, the life of that person is put aside and trodden on like a worthless piece of garbage. Why oh why would we presume to know better than any other person about any part of their lives?

In his book **"On Becoming a Person"** Carl Rogers first postulated the idea of *Unconditional Positive Regard*. Aimed at therapists as a way to approach every client that walks through their door, Rogers extolled the virtue of placing no judgement upon that person so that they had space to open up to that therapist. Unconditional Positive Regards gives rise to the idea that a person is not their actions, not their behaviours nor their emotions. They are a human being with a soul, a spirit and a right to be seen as just that.

Why would we treat anyone differently to that? Even if we are not therapists, coaches, practitioners or helpers, we are all human beings with a soul and a spirit and each of us deserves the right of space.

I believe that being judgemental is poisonous and I also believe the truth to be (and this is of course my own opinion) that when we judge someone we leave some of that poison inside of ourselves. We were born as empty beings, we certainly were not born with judgements waiting inside to be extolled at the first person we meet. What changed?

Actually it doesn't matter what changed, what matters is that it can change back for being judgemental is nothing more than a choice we make and therefore being non-judgemental is a choice as well.

If I were to ask you to approach everyone you meet with an attitude of Unconditional Positive Regard could you do it? You could, of course you could..... After all it is a choice! You now have that choice, you can choose to continue poisoning yourself with the judgement you place on others or you can choose to free yourself with an attitude of unconditional positive regard.

It might not be easy at first, but with practice comes a natural flow that will take over your life. If you are already practicing this then you will know the freedom of soul and spirit that this approach, this choice brings. If you are committed to making the shift then I honour you for taking steps to make your life better.

"Judge not lest you be judged" a certain book once said. Some may always judge you, but you have a choice to not judge in return!

Leave Judgement Aside!

EVOLUTION POINT NUMBER SIX

Notice the Small Things

"Happiness hides in life's small details. If you are not looking, it becomes invisible"

-   *Joyce Brothers*

Notice the Small Things

NLife is busy isn't it? From the moment we rise to the moment we fall we can be completely wrapped up in the day-to-day goings on of a frantic existence. Work, family, friends, social media, TV and any other distraction seeking out our attention and taking our time away.

It is often said that time is the most valuable commodity we have, in the fact that we are limited to a certain number of hours a day and a certain number of days in our lives. We often want to cram stuff in so that we get every experience that we can because none of us know just how long we are here for.

As I sit here writing this book for you it is just over two years since my best friend passed away in his sleep. At just Forty Six years old he was, at the time, a couple of years older than me and in the blink of an eye he was gone. He went to bed one night, apparently with everything ok and simply did not wake in the morning.

Having known him for well over twenty years we had been through much together and had great memories of experiences that could never be replaced. He was the best man at my wedding, we had been to concerts and events together and we had played in a band together. Despite all of those amazing memories do you know what I miss the most? He and I sat in a coffee shop chatting about life!

At the time those simple little chats were enjoyable and yet didn't seem as important as the gigs, concerts, events, football matches and everything else we did. However, sitting here now, it is those small moments of time that I would give anything for again. I miss my friend!

When you can find joy, love and excitement in the smallest of things it becomes much easier to find them in the biggest of things. Going out for a walk and marvelling at the beauty in a tiny flower, watching the majestic beauty of a sunrise or sunset, breathing in deeply and getting the scent of a flower or maybe something sweet being cooked nearby. These are all experiences that we pass up every day as we rush through our lives trying to stuff every day as full as we can...... if only we stuffed it full of the little things!

Each of us is a miracle, a moment of magic in which the universe decided that we were worthy of life and each moment of our life is worthy of enjoying. As you go about your daily life take just a brief moment to appreciate something small and enjoy it fully. As you do so my bet is that you'll add more of those small moments to your day for it is in those tiniest of moments that our lives become something more.

You could even set your watch or phone to chime on the hour, every hour, and choose in that moment to reside in the smallest of things for a short time.

Contained in those moments and those smallest of things is the zest of life, it is there where life has most meaning.

Notice the Small Things.

EVOLUTION POINT NUMBER SEVEN

Make Meditation a Habit

"The goal of Meditation is not to get rid of thoughts or emotions, the goal is to become more aware of your thoughts and emotions and learn how to move through them without getting stuck"

- *Dr. P Goldin*

Make Meditation a Habit

Make Meditation a Habit
I recently read a report that stated that, to date, there have been over 1700 scientific and medical studies on the benefits of meditation and EVERY ONE of them came back

with positive results! Imagine that, a 100% hit rate that meditation has benefits to both your physical, mental and emotional health, just take that in for a moment.

As a rather large generalisation, but quite an accurate one, the person we take care of the least in this world is ourselves. Is that true for you too? Because of this, meditation takes a back seat in many people's lives even if they know how important it is. There is always someone else to help out first; wife, husband, spouse, children, dog, cat..... You know the story right?

What if I were to tell you that those ten to fifteen minutes spent in meditation would help you to take care of those others more effectively than you ever thought possible? Just fifteen minutes of meditation gives us so much freedom in our mind and body that we have more clarity of thought and energy of action.

Very often we become bogged down with everything we have to do in our everyday lives that we cannot think straight due to focussing on one hundred things at once. This leads to a clogged up mind which leads to a massive drain on our physical energy as well as our emotional energy. Tiredness creeps over us and, all of a sudden, we are doing things on autopilot and they are not getting done effectively.

Meditation not only helps us to clear the mind, it helps us to focus our attention on what is important. With clarity comes energy, with energy comes enjoyment, with enjoyment comes happiness. I honestly believe that my daily meditation practice increases my productivity in a day by a factor of five...... that fifteen minutes is invaluable.

Meditation is a skill that needs to be practiced and like any other skill it takes time to form the habit of practice. Depending on which report you read it could take you between twenty one and sixty two days to form a habit. However many days it takes to form that habit in your life it is a small number compared to the years of benefits that will follow from continuing along your meditation journey.

The great thing about technology today is that we have access to so many resources that we are only a moment away from what we need. Whether you want to buy an app on your phone or tablet for guided meditation, get free videos on YouTube, listen to a meditation podcast or get an online course in meditation..... Everything you need is at your fingertips.

Let's cover all bases here shall we, how about making a commitment for the next 2 months (60 days) to spend a minimum of ten minutes a day practicing meditation, you can commit to that can't you? If you don't feel like you have ten minutes in the day then set your alarm for ten minutes earlier or go to bed ten minutes later..... Make a commitment!

As you start to practice, you'll see and feel the benefits working their way into your life and by the time the habit is formed you will never want to go back.

Go on........

Make Meditation a Habit!

EVOLUTION POINT NUMBER EIGHT

Love Rules - Understand Them

"The best and most beautiful things in this world cannot be seen or even heard, but must be felt with the heart"

-   *Helen Keller*

Love Rules - Understand Them!

If I were to ask you the following question:

"What has to happen for you to feel loved?"

Would you know the answer? Would you consider that important information to know?

What if I were to ask you:

"What has to happen for your wife / husband (or significant other) to feel loved?"

Would you know the answer to that one? That's some hugely important information isn't it?

Imagine, just for a moment, that you knew exactly how to make your significant other feel completely and utterly loved at any time you choose to do so. Imagine that they have had a tough day at work or that the kids have been getting on top of them and that, in that moment, you could drastically alter their emotional state and have them feeling totally loved by you. How powerful would that be to their life? What if they could do the same for you? How powerful would that be for your life?

We each have rules set up, completely unconsciously, for how we feel any emotion and those rules can be discovered at a conscious level and used to our advantage. At some point in our past we had an experience that was so powerful that we unconsciously decided that it was in those steps that we would connect that emotion. It is within those steps that we can discover how to make both ourselves and the ones we love feel loved. We just have to discover those steps!

I'll ask you to revisit the question I asked above and take the time to consider it deeply and then answer it consciously:

"What has to happen for you to feel loved?"
I know it may seem strange to start with but when you take some time to consider it you'll discover a set of steps that lead to that feeling of love overtaking your entire system. Go on, take seven minutes now to consider the answers to the question and write down all the steps.

Now that you have done that I highly recommend having the same conversation with your spouse so that you know what has to happen for them to feel loved. Tell them why you are doing it, explain the process as I have explained it to you above and then discover the love rules........ Life will never be the same again.

Let me give you an example:

Here's a list of my wife's live rules, in the order that they need to happen:

1. Look deeply and gently into her eyes
2. Whisper softly to her "I love you"
3. Hold her close

...... et voila...... she feels completely loved by me in that moment! How often do you think I use that sequence? That's right, I use it often so that she always feels loved by me!

How often would you use your spouse's love rules so that they know how much you love them?

"So how do I find them Graham?" - I can hear you shouting!

It's simple, follow the question above, have the conversation and pay close attention to what they say. Then test it out! If it's not quite right, carry on with the conversation and get more pointers and then try them out. Eventually you'll discover the rules and you'll know exactly what to do to make your loved one feel..... Loved!!

If you truly love someone, how much time would you spend on learning how to make them feel completely loved at any moment? Would you take 30 minutes? An hour maybe? Or would you take all the time that is needed? When we are entirely in love time doesn't matter does it. Effort and energy come easily so that we can be a part of the joy of their lives and they being a part of theirs.

There's a song lyric that I love by Richie Sambora that goes:

Honey, honey don't you understand,
To make you feel like a woman,
Makes me feel like a man.

This is love isn't it? Making the other person in your life feel loved. I would go so far as to say that to truly feel loved yourself you first need to know how to make someone else feel loved.

Know the Love Rules...... and understand them!

EVOLUTION POINT NUMBER NINE

Take Care of You First

"To fall in love with yourself is the first secret to happiness"

-    *Robert Monley*

Take Care of Your First

It seems that, for some reason, self care and self love have become a bad thing in our society and I have no idea why. Honestly, how did it ever start that we shouldn't love ourselves? Why would that be the case?

I can't claim to be any different, for many years I had absolutely no love for myself and in fact at points I would truly dislike myself. I would berate myself, talk to myself in the horriblest of ways and not take care of my health.... Either physical, mental or emotional!

Was it a lack of self worth, self esteem or a feeling of not being good enough? It could well have been all three at some points. What I discovered was two-fold:

Firstly, we cannot truly have love for another unless we have love for ourselves first. To quote Dr. Wayne Dyer "you cannot give away what you don't have" - no truer words spoken.

Secondly, I discovered that this is not who we are meant to be. We are not born with any sort of self loathing or worthlessness inside, they are instilled overtime. Who we are meant to be is loving, caring, compassionate beings on a journey to discover ourselves. When we look inside to who we really are we will uncover the truth about ourselves and it is never malicious in any way.

If I were to ask you - "Who are you?" and said that you should make two lists, one starting with "I am" and the other with "I am a" what would you put down. An important point here is that behaviours and emotions are not who we are so they cannot be included in the list. Things like "I am lazy" are not appropriate as Laziness is a behaviour. "I am stressed" or "I am angry" are emotional states that come and go and therefore not who you are at your core.

When you discover who you are at your core it is easy to take care of yourself more, it is easier to love yourself more......... I wonder, as I am writing this, whether it is our behaviours and emotions that we don't love and as they tend to be at the surface we only ever notice them until we go looking deeper.

Let's be honest here for a second shall we, your chances of being here today, of actually being born were millions to one..... MILLIONS! At the point where that magical, miraculous point happened and that everything aligned, you were chosen. At that point you were worthy of life, you were good enough to be given the chance of life. What has happened since has no bearing on what happens next, the only thing that matters right here and right now as you are reading this page is that you were born worthy and good enough............. And you still are.

What would you need to find important in life to make you take care of yourself and love yourself? Would you need to find your physical health important? What about your mental and emotional health? What about your growth as a human being so that you were striving to be a better version of you each day? Would you need to find it important to contribute to others so that you knew you were doing some good in the world?

What would you need to find important?

Now that you know, you have the chance to focus on those things and make your life yours, a self loving, self caring life. There is nothing selfish about this by the way; let me tell you a little story.

Have you ever been on a plane? Even if you haven't you will have seen it on TV where the stewards and stewardesses take the time before take off to show you where the emergency exits are. During that safety demonstration they always tell you about the oxygen masks dropping from above your head if the cabin decompresses and that you should put your mask on first before helping others.

Now, if you are a parent this is incredibly hard to hear because you want to make sure you children are safe first. The truth though is that if you go to help them first and the cabin decompresses you might not be able to breathe to help them and you could all die. Whereas if you slip your oxygen mask on first you can then help them as you can still breathe.

It's a bit of a harsh example but it is exactly the reason you are told to put your mask on first. Why then, would we not care for ourselves first so that we can care more effectively for others? Why would we not love ourselves first so we can have a deeper love for others?

Making you a priority, taking care of you first is not wrong and it is the most natural thing to do......... we just seem to have forgotten that in our society. So I have a question for you (I know, I ask a lot of questions!):

What will you do today to take care of yourself a little better?

Remember: Take Care of Your First!

EVOLUTION POINT NUMBER TEN

Be Outside More

"Spending time in nature has a way of nurturing the soul"

\-   *Katrina Mayer*

Be Outside More

Have you noticed how 'inside' our lives are these days? We just seem to do everything inside don't we? We wake up inside, we travel to work inside a car, we work inside, we eat lunch inside, we exercise inside, we travel home inside that same car, we eat dinner inside, we watch TV inside, we play games with our children inside and eventually we go to bed again inside.

That's a whole lot of inside!!!

Now, before you start shouting at me via this book and saying ..... "What, you want me to SLEEP outside Graham?????" No, of course not (unless you really feel like it).

What I am saying here is that we are outside beings, we should be outside in the world not trapped away in a box, staring at a box all day! We should be outside, enjoying the elements in whatever form they come, sun, rain, snow...... these are our natural places to spend time. It doesn't matter if you live in the country and can roam around wide open fields or you live in the city and can roam around wide open streets. The outside is who we are.

Of course, there are studies that show that spending time in nature is good for us. It relaxes us, it helps us to breath, it calms our system and refreshes our soul, but if you are not close to nature does that mean you don't bother?

As I sit here now (inside!) I'm sitting in my office and it's 7:15am, I've already been out for a walk with my dog Charlie and I can't imagine not doing that every single morning. The first thing I want to do when I raise myself up out of bed is to get outside, to breathe some fresh air, to feel the chill wind against my face (It's autumn in the UK as I'm writing this and it's raining!) and to get my body and entire system moving.

What would I do at 5:00am when I get up if I didn't go for a walk with Charlie? Sit and watch TV? Listen to the radio? Start work? All inside pursuits right? Not for me, I prefer the outside as it lifts my soul...... even in the rain.

If you don't get up and go for a walk outside each day why not try it for one month. Get up a little earlier each day and walk for somewhere between 30 - 45 minutes each day. Take the time to look, listen and feel everything around you as you walk and completely take it in. Breathe deeply as your morning stroll continues and let your entire system kick start itself, ready for the rest of the day. It might be tough to start with if you haven't walked in the morning before, but keep at it and I know you'll learn to love it. Being outside is not only good for our well-being, it is also imperative for our wholebeing. Our wholebeing is about discovering that we are not only connected as an individual internally but also that we are connected to everything and everyone around us.

Imagine, as you walk along that you walk past a beautiful rose bush that is in full bloom. The colours of the flowers strike you, they open your eyes to the beauty that nature offers in our world. Just as you are taking in the beauty that's in front of you, suddenly you get the faintest of wisps of the smell coming from that rose and you go in closer to breathe in more of that odour. You take a huge breathe in through your nose and the glorious smell emanating from that rose takes you away just for a moment. You close your eyes and you and suddenly somewhere else, somewhere beautiful.

Are you connected to that rose? Could you see it and maybe even smell it as I described it to you? When we discover our wholebeing we discover that we are connected to everyone and everything around us. This opens the door to enjoying the outside even more for just as we are connected to everything and everyone, knowing that fosters a deeper connection with ourselves.

Consider, for a moment, when else could you be outside each day? Could you walk or cycle to work? Could you go for a quick walk at lunchtime? Could you exercise outside rather than in a gym? Are you in a country that has the weather to allow you to eat dinner outside? Rather than watching TV could you sit outside and read a book?

The message is a simple one..... Find ways to Be Outside More!

EVOLUTION POINT NUMBER ELEVEN

Read Whatever Takes You

"Books are the plane, and the train, and the road. They are the destination and the journey. They are home"

\-   *Anna Quindlen*

Read Whatever Takes You

Are you a reader? Do you like to read or love to read? Do you take a book slowly to enjoy it or do you devour it in a night? Maybe you pick up a book but never finish it or you just read what you can?

Whichever of these is right for you, it's just great that you read!

I've heard many experts and 'so-called' gurus tell people that they must read a certain type of book..... It must be a book on personal development, it must be a book on success, it must be a book on business, it must be a book on making money......

UTTER RUBBISH!

A book is personal to you and your choices, a book is time out from your normal daily routine, a book is a time to escape the world just for a short time. For me, getting time to read is about having time with me and that is something we all struggle with these days isn't it. There are so many people demanding our time and attention that just fifteen minutes of reading can seem like a blissful escape, a holiday almost.

There was a study I read many years ago that said, of the people who bought personal development books, only 18% ever opened them and read the first page! Eighteen Percent!!!! That means 72% of those people never even bothered to read word one..... What?????? These people must have bookshelves full of books they have never read, what a waste?

As I sit here writing that I'm reminded of just how grateful I am that you have decided to open this book and that you have got this far.... Thank You!

My honest opinion is that people get pressured into buying these books but never read them because they don't know where to start and so fear kicks in. They look at their bookshelves, or their catalogue on a reading device, and are overwhelmed so they simply don't bother.

Here's my solution, it is your choice if you choose to follow it.

I think we should read whatever takes us away in that moment and mix it up a bit between genres. This way we don't overload our mind with the same information, or the same type of information, we open it up to new things all the time. We give our minds space to discover something new and time to process it. Whether it be factual information, personal development, or a work of fiction, it doesn't matter. We should read whatever takes us away in that moment.

To give you an example from my own reading, I might read something spiritual (Metahuman by Deepak Chopra has just come out as I'm writing this and that is the next book I'm diving into!). Then I might something of fiction in nature, I'm a fan of the James Patterson novels and in particular his Alex Cross series. Then I might read something that involves my work to upskill myself, so it might be something on Life Coaching, NLP, Hypnotherapy or a Complementary Therapy. I'm also a fan of Stephen King so I might read one of his novels.

I read whatever takes me away in that moment and there's often times that I have two books on the go at once. Why? Because I can read whatever I am in the mood for and I know that at any given time I could be in the mood for either. They take me away for that fifteen to twenty minutes and allow me to just be. Not do, just be!

Not do, just be!

Read Whatever Takes You!

EVOLUTION POINT NUMBER TWELVE

Enjoy the Silence

"The most significant conversations of our lives occur in silence"

- *Simon Van Booy*

Enjoy the Silence

Do you have someone in your life that always has to fill the silence? You know the sort of person, the one that just can't stand it and has to say something! If you've got children then I'm guessing you know what I'm talking about. Certainly my daughter has been like that (although she is getting better as I teach her more) so I feel your pain!

Are you like that? Do you not like silence and if not what stops you from just being in the moment of quiet?

A little while ago I added a quote to my Facebook group which had a very good response as people realised the truth behind it, here it is:

"The doors to the solutions for all of life's problems open inwards"

Just take a moment to let that settle in and start to resonate throughout your system, what does it say to you? When I came up with it I wanted to convey the truth that all of your problems are solved by looking inside yourself and the only way you can truly look inside yourself is in moments of silence. That moment of quiet, where your mind isn't distracted by all the noise going on outside, and inside, is the moment when truth comes through.

Let's be absolutely clear about this, it takes practice to enjoy the silence..... It takes practice to be silent and be comfortable with it. Our lives are filled with noise and distraction and everything is vying for our attention. We have gotten into the habit of instant gratification by being able to get everything at the touch of a button, the very moment we think about it.

Enjoying the silence is at the opposite end of that spectrum, it's not an instant gratification thing. It takes time, practice and effort as do all the worthwhile things in this world. What it brings to us far outweighs any instant gratification solution you will ever find.

In this book we have already discussed two areas that will help you to enjoy the silence and seek the answers to any problem. Meditation is the perfect practice to learn to love the process and when you combine that with the Heart Activation Breathing, that I mentioned in the Breathe Effectively chapter, you have the key to truth.

People need to stop looking to the media, social media and on-line searches to answer their problems and learn to go inside and bask in the silence. If I were to do a search on a leading search engine for the answer to any problem I would get thousands of answers within a millisecond and most of them would conflict with each other. Why? Because everyone is different and everyone has their own theories and answers but the only true answer is inside and in the silence.

Life Coaches, Therapists and Helping Practitioners know the value of silence and often use it as time to let their clients think and discover the answers they seek. That space to just be in the moment creates more solutions than any other realm of helping.

The answers reside within, the answers reside in the moment.

Enjoy the Silence!

EVOLUTION POINT NUMBER THIRTEEN

Connect to the Higher You

"When you contact the Higher Self, the source of power within, you tap into a reservoir of infinite power"

\- *Deepak Chopra*

Connect to The Higher You

C The first step in connecting to the higher you is to acknowledge that it is there. Whatever you may call this higher self it is important to recognise and accept its existence. You may call it God (or another religious figure), it might be the

Universe, you may call it Source (as Dr. Wayne Dyer did as part of his work with the Tao te Ching), it may be *The Mind* and see it as part of a collective consciousness or you may just see it as a higher consciousness. Whatever it is to you, just know that it is there and it always has your back.

In his book "Change Your Thoughts, Change Your Mind", Dr. Dyer states that part of the Tao te Ching says that this part of you cannot be named for the moment you name it is the moment it becomes a 'thing' and yet it has no substance in this world so cannot be named. For now I will use the term Higher Self to refer to the power that sits there unassuming.

We have already discussed, in this book, the part that Meditation, Breathing and Silence have to play in transforming your life in this Life Evolution. These are all part of the equation to connecting to the Higher Self.

The Higher Self is where the answers come from, where truth resides and where the true core of you is born and lives from. It is the core of everything wonderful within you and it is the place that can answer any questions you have while helping to resolve all issues. It is also the part that many people close off, shut down and refuse to admit exists through fear of the unknown. Yet the unknown is not to be feared, it is to be embraced as it is only by going into the unknown do we ever advance as human beings.

As you start to practice Meditation, Breathing and enjoying the Silence (or continue to do so if you are already doing this) then you can start to connect. You can start to have conversations with that part of yourself that has the answers you are seeking, that will always tell you the truth. We are often taught that talking to ourselves and listening to our inner voice is bad and we are often told that if we 'hear voices' we must be ready for the funny farm. Nothing could be further from the truth, it is that conversation internally and extending to the Higher Self that provides the deepest and most meaningful of chats.

Many people around the world know that the only way to make an important decision is to meditate on it and ask the question of that Higher Self. They know that if they are conflicted about something it is that Higher Self that has the answers they seek. They instinctively know that the Higher Self has a power and energy all of its own that transcends any physical barrier we might place upon ourselves. Within that realm there are now barriers, no limiting beliefs and no fears that are insurmountable. The realm of the Higher Self is all empowering, magical and miraculous where anything is possible.

For me, connecting to that place of Higher Self is getting in tune with the Universe, matching the frequency of my soul to that of a place where everything is connected. Its like seeing the brushstrokes on the biggest picture ever imagined, hearing the most beautiful song ever heard and feeling a vibration that moves your core. In this place I feel connected to myself, to those around me and to the universe all at the same time. It is like I am tapping into a flowing river that can carry me anywhere I choose to go.

I'm sure you remember me talking about instant gratification...... this isn't one of those things! This takes time and practice, it takes faith and commitment, it takes every part of you.

Meditate, Breathe, be Silent and Connect to the Higher You!

EVOLUTION POINT NUMBER FOURTEEN

Know Your Chargers and Drains

"Do more of what sets your life alight and less of what dims your light and make sure you know the difference"

\-   *Graham Nicholls*

Know your Chargers and Drains

What is the thing that sets your soul on fire? What lights you up like a bulb on maximum wattage? What charges you like the world's most powerful solar panel?

If I asked you to, could you provide me a list of twenty things that really get you going, that light your fire and give you energy? What about if I asked you to list twenty things that drain the energy out of you quicker than a bucket with a huge hole in it drains water? Most people can give me a list of the stuff that drains them, it seems that we all know what tires us out and we can provide that list without thinking. However, ask people to provide the same length list of things that get them going, that switch them on, and they struggle.

Try it the next time you are having a conversation with someone. Ask them to tell you what tires them out and drains their energy and see how many things they can come up with in two minutes. Then ask them what really energises them and see how many examples they have in that same 2 minute period. My bet is that it won't even be half the list!

Why is it that we focus on those negative areas? Do you know something, this isn't the place for that discussion. What this is, is the place for is discovering the positives, uncovering the powerful and finding those chargers. So for a moment or two, take the time to consider your list of chargers and add as many as you can. Just like having more plug sockets in your home gives you more chance to charge your mobile phone, having more things that charge you up gives you a greater chance of being charged.

When you know what your drains are you can avoid them or at least minimise them in your life and when you know what charges your very core you can ensure you find them anywhere. Write them both down and commit them to memory, make sure you know that in every day that comes along you have chargers ready and waiting.

Let me make this clear, this is not about doing a balancing act! If you were to sit your drains and chargers on either side of a metaphorical set of scales you chargers need to MASSIVELY outweigh your drains. Like a boxing match that lasts but a few seconds, your chargers should knock your drains out for the count.

Simply put, do more of what charges you and less of what drains you so that you always have the energy to live your life and make sure that you know the difference between the two.
Whether it be physical chargers, mental chargers or emotional chargers, make sure you know what they are and use them often. We build habits through repetition and a habit of charging will serve you much more than a habit of drains. Which do you have an abundance of at the moment? Which will you have an abundance of going forward?

Life equals energy, you can either have that energy drained from you or charged into you...... the choice is yours.

Know Your Chargers and Drains!

EVOLUTION POINT NUMBER FIFTEEN

Be Creative Daily

"You can't use up your creativity. The more you use, the more you have"

- *Maya Angelou*

Be Creative Daily

Be Creative Daily

When we humans lived in caves, we had to find things to eat, there were no shops or supermarkets, there was no pizza delivery and there was no fast food joints. What did we do? We got creative! We discovered how to create tools in order to dig up plants, weapons in order to catch animals and kill them, we used our creativity without even knowing what creativity was.

The problem is that at some point in history we discovered what creativity is and a little knowledge is a dangerous thing (as someone probably once said!). Have you ever noticed that the moment we know we have a certain skill or ability someone says that they don't have it! It's amazing that people will argue with you and say that they don't have that particular skill even if it is a natural part of who we are as human beings.

We are born with creativity, it is in every essence of our being and is a completely natural part of who we are. People are just creative in different areas and that's a great thing..... Imagine if we were all creative in just one area - we might all play music and do nothing else! Ok so that's a personal one as I love music but it's not my point of creativity. I'm creative in the manner of writing and developing things to help others. Writing books like this one, creating online video courses in Life Coaching and many other similar subjects, that is where my creativity lives.

For all of you out there that think you are not creative, consider what you might be creative in and what you enjoy doing. Do you enjoy playing a musical instrument, drawing, painting, cooking, DIY, gardening, working with animals, teaching or raising children. Oh and by the way, if you have raised children, or are currently raising children, you can't tell me that you are not creative! You have to be one of the most creative people in the world to raise a child and teach them life's lessons while playing with them, cleaning up after them and generally entertaining them!

Whatever your area of creativity, you need to use it daily! Using our creative side sets us free for a while, it allows our minds to roam far away from the day to day grind that we invariably get ourselves into. Set aside some time each day, even if it is only fifteen to twenty minutes and let yourself go. Ask yourself *"what I am I going to use my creativity for today?"* and then let yourself go.

Now, with our busy day to day lives we can sometimes get stuck in thinking about everything else and this traps our creativity inside. Don't worry..... You are in luck! You see you have already learned a couple of key skills that will help you to free up that creative side. You have learned how important breathing is and, particularly, you learned about Heart Activation Breathing. Heart Activation Breathing connects mind and heart and brings out the true you and there is no truer (is that a word?) part of you than the creative side. A good place to start!

However, there is another step you can take with the Heart Activation Breathing that really opens up that creative side. Because you have learned how to breathe into one specific area of your body (Heart) you know how to breathe into any area of your body. Once you have been breathing into your heart for three to five minutes ask yourself *"where does my creativity come from?"* and naturally let your hand come to rest on that area, wherever it is. Now move your focus to breathing into this area, you are now breathing life into your creativity!

Start to let you creativity flow as you breathe life into it, allow it to vibrate through you and work into every part of you. Allow it to naturally flow to your mind, your soul, your body and then let it free. Open your eyes and do whatever feels right in that moment; write, draw, paint, talk......... create!

The energy, freedom and flow that being creative gives you is like nothing else. It has a way of sparking your entire being and why would you not want to ignite your spark every day?

Be Creative Daily!

EVOLUTION POINT
NUMBER SIXTEEN

Compare to Nobody

"Personality begins where comparison leaves off. Be Unique. Be Memorable. Be Confident. Be Proud."

\- *Shannon L. Adler*

Compare to Nobody

Let's get this out of the way right at the start of this chapter..... You are you, you were born to be you, you were destined to be you and the only person you should ever be is YOU.

I call it **The Comparison Cage**, it is where we put ourselves the moment we compare ourselves to anyone else. We trap ourselves in a tiny little cage and struggle to find a way out. At that point of thinking we should be like anyone else we dim our own light a little and the longer it goes on the more our flame dies. The key to that cage seems to be out of reach no matter how much we struggle for it, all because we think someone else has it better than us!

Have you ever noticed how we only compare ourselves to those that we perceive as having a better life than us? Don't you find it strange that we don't look at someone else who is having a truly horrible time and say *"hmmmm I wish I was in their shoes"*? Surely if we are to compare ourselves to those we perceive to have things better than we do then it's only fair to compare to those that don't right? No, we wouldn't do that would we!

The truth is that you don't know everything about their lives, you only know what you see on the surface. They may appear to have more money than you, or a better career, or a bigger house, or nicer cars but NONE of that matters. So what if they do? If you want that you will NEVER get it while you are looking at their life and bemoaning how 'lucky' they are. As long as you stay in that Comparison Cage you are trapped and will never get to where you are supposed to be.

There is, however, one person that you absolutely SHOULD compare yourself to.... YOU! The you of yesterday to be precise, when you take a look at the you of yesterday do you see that you have moved forward? Do you see that you have grown? If not then it's time to start working towards the you of tomorrow so that when you look back on today you'll know you are a better version of you. That is all we can ever strive for, to be a better version of yourself today than you were yesterday and to be a better version tomorrow again.

In whichever area you want to change and improve your life make sure to take small steps daily. Create a little improvement every single day and you will be surprised how far you can move within a year. Imagine standing on a straight road, the tarmac is laid out in front of you so that you can see into the distance. Your average step forward is probably around 1 metre and you start to walk forwards counting your paces as you go. When you get to 365 steps you stop and look back, you see how far you've come.... Quite a distance right? Here's the thing, some days you will take more than one step forwards in your life, you might take three or four because things are flying along for you, some days you will just take one. All of a sudden, those 365 steps have turned into 500........ Now look back and see how far you have come, simply by only comparing yourself and not others!

There's a Tony Robbins quote that goes *"Most people overestimate what they can do in a year and underestimate what they can do in five years"* - I prefer to think that most people don't know just how much they can accomplish by just taking a step a day and then a few steps on good days. As long as they are YOUR steps and only your steps!

Later in this book I will be offering you a chance to move yourself forward with the Challenge365 process, I hope you'll join in!

For now though......... Compare to Nobody!

EVOLUTION POINT NUMBER SEVENTEEN

Accept Yourself

"When you accept yourself you are freed from the burden of needing others to accept you. Don't allow anyone or anything to control, limit, repress or discourage you from being your true self"

\- *Steve Maraboli*

ccept Yourself

A Let me start this chapter by clearing one thing up, accepting yourself does not mean accepting where you are now and never moving forward ever again! Honestly, I get that objection so many times when I'm teaching, speaking or coaching..... *"But Graham, if I accept who I am now I'll never change or improve"* - Rubbish!

I would, in fact, go so far as to say that to change or improve yourself, your life and your current situation you MUST first accept yourself. You see it is that self acceptance that sets you free to become more and to do more. While you continue to be un-accepting of who you are then you trap yourself behind the walls of the stories that you create to keep you in place.

Accepting yourself is the natural progression from comparing to nobody, once you drop those comparison traps you have only you left to compare yourself to. When you accept yourself you stop seeking acceptance from anyone else and the connection of not comparing and not seeking acceptance removes the shackles that have held you back.

Seeking acceptance from others never lasts does it? You may get acceptance from your boss for doing a great job one day but the next day is just another day and you have to start all over again. You might get acceptance from your friends for helping them out but the next time they need help and you can't give it you feel like the acceptance has fallen away (whether it has or not). You see, acceptance from others is temporary.... Why? Because it is a feeling within you! It's not what they do or say, it's not how they act, it's not whether they call or text you and it's not whether they praise you.

Acceptance from others is a feeling that you construct and because of that it is flimsy in nature and destroyed easily.

The difference between acceptance from others and accepting yourself is simple..... Accepting yourself is a one time deal! That's right, you only truly accept yourself once and when you have that acceptance never goes away. Self acceptance is there for life, it's in it for the long haul, it is your lifelong companion and it's one of the greatest companions you'll ever have.

We are misguided by life and the people that make up our life as we told that to be 'happy' we must be a certain way and do certain things. Society, the education system, the media and social media all preach the same thing. You MUST get a good education, you MUST get a good job and work to advance up the career ladder, you MUST get married and have a family, you MUST buy a house, you MUST, you MUST, you MUST. Who on earth ever decided that we should all do the same thing and follow the same path? While those things might be right for some people they are not right for everyone.

The only thing (in my humble opinion) that we MUST do is be ourselves and to be ourselves we must accept who we are and not who the world is trying to force us to be.

Self acceptance is a journey, it is a path that we must choose and stay on even when times get tough. It's all too easy to fall off the path and return to our prescribed lives when we find things we don't like or when fear shows up. Yet that path to self acceptance is the path to freedom.

The journey starts by opening up to who is buried deep inside, that person you were meant to be when you were born. You were born worthy of life and worthy of living that life as the universe only gives worth to the world. At the point you came into this world you also had everything you needed to live whatever life you wanted, you had enough and you always were enough.

These two things, being worthy and being enough, are always within us and yet so many allow those two lights to be diminished inside of themselves. They allow their circumstances of life get to them and weaken the flames of worth and enough. Yet, when we go inside and journey towards discovering our truest of selves we find worth and enough waiting for us. They never gave up on us even if we gave up on them, they simply sat there waiting to be found again and they are found through acceptance.

Close off your brain for a while my friends and go inside your heart for it is there that your truth resides. While the brain is filled with the stories and experiences of your life thus far, your heart holds the true you. When you travel to the very centre of your being you open up a world that you have only seen glimpses of as the true you attempts to break through. You see, you are always there and you can be found again through connecting deeply to your heart.

Stop for a moment and do the following exercise if you will, read through it first and then follow the simple instructions. Alternatively you could have someone read it to you:

1. Close your eyes and focus solely on your breathing for just a few moments. Notice your chest and abdomen expanding as you breath in and then contract again as you breathe out. Focus only on your breathing.
2. Now shift your focus to noticing your clothing against your skin. Pick any area of your body and notice how you clothing lays softly against your skin and become aware that you hadn't noticed it until right now when you focussed on it.
3. Notice what your hands are touching, is it this book or are they resting comfortably? Notice whatever they are touching and what it feels like, you can even move your fingers gently to feel the texture and temperature. Focus in on it for a few seconds and notice everything about it.
4. Finally, without moving, notice your pulse. Some people feel their heart beating while others feel the pulse softly in the ends of their fingers or toes. Wherever you notice it just pay attention to it for a few seconds and notice it's calming rhythm. Become aware that you had never noticed this sensation before and

yet you can be still and feel your heart giving each and every area of your body life.

Even though you don't place your focus on your heart beating and your pulse thumping away, they are always there doing their job and keeping you alive. Yet when you do focus on them you can find them quite easily and know that they are there..... Go on, try it again now! Close your eyes and focus on your pulse, there it is again waiting for you!

Just like your heartbeat and pulse are waiting for you, so is your true self! The you that is worthy of living any sort of life you choose, the you that is good enough to be who you want to be. The true you is inside that heartbeat and you are found through the journey to self acceptance and once that journey begins and those doors open you'll know you are on the right path.

If you remember nothing else from this chapter or this entire book please remember this one thing:

You were born worthy of a wondrous life and you were born good enough to live it!

Accept Yourself - always!

EVOLUTION POINT NUMBER EIGHTEEN

Let go of accomplishment

"We all obsess about what we are doing and accomplishing.What if we let it go and simply made the way we live our lives our accomplishment"

\- *Maria Shriver*

L et go of Accomplishment

It is one of life's greatest lies, that we need to constantly and consistently seek to accomplish something bigger and better. That we should go after a better job or promotion, that we should earn a certain amount of money, that we should buy the big house and drive the fancy, expensive car.

Don't get me wrong here, I have no problem with having the drive to live the life you want and if you want those things you should go and get them. What I mean by letting go of accomplishment is to not let it define you. Consider something you feel as though you have accomplished in your life and remember, just for a moment, the time that it happened. How did it feel?

If you are picturing it in your head now, or talking yourself through that moment, remember if clearly. Did you celebrate? Did you throw a wild party or did you simply allow yourself a couple of fist pumps with the occasional "yes, get in there" thrown in? Now here's the thing...... how did it feel the following day? How about the following month or the following year? Not quite the same as in that moment right.

The trouble with accomplishing your goals is that once you have accomplished it, it is never enough. That feeling of success soon fades and you have to find something else to chase and accomplish, and then something else, and then something else. The circle becomes endless and you are in peril of losing sight of what is really important in your life.

Making the way we lead our lives our core focus and then adding on reaching our goals as a beautiful addition gives us the freedom to enjoy as many moments as possible. In this way life does not only become about certain moments in which we have a short high only for us to discover that it was still not enough to satisfy. Leading a life not to be accomplished but to be purposeful, with purposeful pursuits, gives us a sense of accomplishment that never fades.

When we make a shift in our lives towards who we can contribute to, who we can grow into and who we can love, we move to a place of consistent purposefulness. In this place we flow towards our goals and they towards us. The actions we take are undertaken with greater ease, joy and fulfilment because we don't need to chase accomplishment, we simply want to achieve something more.

Schools give out certificates and awards to children for doing well but there is no certificate needed to show how they are loved and how they love. Just like those children do not need that 'love certificate', we do not need the 'certificate' of accomplishment. Our lives are worth so much more than that and there is so much more in our lives to celebrate rather than just fist pumping once in a while!

If you must have an accomplishment to chase in your life then make it the accomplishment of living your life on your terms every day. In this way you unconsciously give others around you the freedom to do exactly the same.

Let go of accomplishment!

EVOLUTION POINT NUMBER NINETEEN

Watch out for Inspiration

"Just don't give up on what you really want to do. Where there is love and inspiration I don't think you can go wrong"

- *Ella Fitzgerald*

Watch Out for Inspiration

Have you ever been inspired? You know, that moment when everything just seems to be in perfect flow with you. How often does that happen to you? Is it often, not too often or few and far between?

The Universe never stops sending us inspiration, it is like Niagra Falls pouring from the Universe towards us. We can truly be inspired by anything and everything when the moment catches us. What, though, if we don't have to wait for that moment to catch us? What if we were to watch out for inspiration every single day of our lives and use whatever inspiration we find to keep our lives moving in the right direction. Wouldn't that be great?

Have you ever heard or seen someone being interviewed, an artist, a musician or a writer and they get asked "what inspires you?" The answer can come from anywhere can't it. Musicians draw inspiration from other musicians, whether from their own genre or from another genre of music. They draw inspiration from a certain part of the world or a specific area of the country. World events have been given credit for inspiring whole albums while social unrest and politics can also play their part.

I heard an interview with Billy Joe Armstrong, the lead singer of Green Day, in which he was asked where the inspiration came for the album American Idiot. He said that while the political and social climate at the time was a key factor, the first lines of a particular song came from a walk. He was walking around New York one day with everything that was going on in the world circling his head. As he walked some words came to him that he said excited him and scared him all at the same time:

"I'm the son of rage and love, the Jesus of Suburbia"

From that moment on, he knew he had something special and the album was written from there. Powerful stuff this inspiration isn't it!

I love his description of when those words came to him, the fact that is excited and scared him all at the same time (actually his exact words were a lot more colourful than that). Does that describe inspiration? Should inspiration excite the hell out of you and give you the buzz to get something done, while also adding a little bit of fear into the recipe? Somewhere inside of me I think that's exactly what inspiration should do.

When you get inspired you have the opportunity to do something new or create something new. Even though Green Day had written songs and released albums before they had never written an album like American Idiot. That thought of stepping out and doing or creating something new should have a little fear attached sometimes, it's a healthy fear that signals something great is on the other side of it.

"But Graham," I hear you shout, "where do I get my inspiration from?"

As I mentioned at the start of this chapter, inspiration flows from the Universe to us in more ways than we could ever imagine possible. It flows to us, it surrounds us and it sparks from within us. All you have to do is pay attention and WHAM, something hits you. It might be a metaphorical WHACK in the head that screams WAKE UP! On the other hand, it may be more subtle like an idea that suddenly springs into your mind that, if you don't catch hold of quickly enough, will only be there fleetingly and then gone again.

Within us we have something called the Reticular Activating System (or RAS for short) that notices the things we are paying attention to at that particular time. The old way of thinking about the RAS was this; imagine you are going to buy a new car or a new outfit. You want something different, something not too many people have so you go to a specific place where you have seen one and BOOM..... There it is! You snap it up as quickly as possible and congratulate yourself on having this new item.

On the way home, shock horror, you see someone else with it.... Aaaahhhhhhhhhhh.

What happened? Did everyone suddenly go out and buy this thing at exactly the same time you were buying it? No, they already had it but you didn't see it because you weren't focussed on it until that point. Up until that point your RAS was focussed somewhere else.

The thing with this description of RAS is that it seems to focus only on the things you see. However, the word reticular means to have a form of net or intricate and entangled network which suggests much more than just our vision. What the RAS actually does is captures everything that is in relation to what we are focussing on. Not just what we see but what we hear, what we feel and what we think. It is, without a doubt, one of the most powerful human abilities when used..... And most people don't consciously use it.

When I am preparing to write a book, an article or produce a new course I am looking for inspiration everywhere. I will know the title of the book or course, I'll know what it is about and then I start to pay attention to anything and everything that might hold inspiration for a section of it. I might grab an idea from something I read, see or hear, then again a feeling may come over me that I should take more time to consider this or that, and I pay attention. I carry a notebook with me so that, if a thought should occur, that I think will be a source of inspiration, I can write it down and revisit later.

The other important aspect of my process is that I meditate with the particular subject in mind. I'll close in on that subject and think only of that, noticing the thoughts that crop up and investigating them throughout the meditation. This way I am not just approaching this at a conscious level, I am also opening up my subconscious mind so that it knows my area of focus. With all of that in place inspiration comes.

Why does it come? Because I have activated the parts of me that will notice and grab hold of the inspiration that the Universe sends my way. I have decided, both consciously and unconsciously, to pay attention.

The Universe offers these gifts every single day.

Watch out for Inspiration!

EVOLUTION POINT NUMBER TWENTY

Take Action Every Day

"Take Action! An inch of movement will bring you closer to your goals than a mile of intention"

\-   *Steve Maraboli*

Take Action Every Day

Have you heard of the Law of Attraction? There was a book and movie / documentary that came out about it a few years back. In this book and documentary they authors gave three steps to activating the Law of Attraction........ But they missed one!

You see, this book would have us believe that to have whatever we want all we have to do is ask for it, believe it will happen and then sit back and wait for the glory to arrive..... Rubbish! Let's say you want to start a new business and you want that business to be wildly successful. You spell out exactly what you want to happen, you write it all down in intricate details and you create a belief inside you that this will actually happen and then you sit back and wait.

BUT...... by sitting back and waiting you have stalled even before getting started. Who is going to start your business if not you? Who will create the inventory, website, and get the social media going if not you? If you do not take action then you do not get what you want.

Let's look at another example..... You decide you want to be fit and healthy, you are determined that your lifestyle should be as healthy as it can be and you want to lose 30 pounds in weight. You follow the Law of Attraction plan, write it all down, be specific about what exactly you want and then believe that it will happen and sit back and wait.

How many pounds do you think you will lose sitting on that couch? How will your health improve if you don't change your eating and exercise habits? What will happen? Nothing, Nada, Zilch, Zip, Zero!

Nothing happens if we don't take the actions to make it happen, we won't get healthier and the business won't start itself. You won't get that new job or the step up on the career ladder and that new car you want...... not happening! Unless you take action and take action every single day.

There's a quote by Tony Robbins that states:

"People overestimate what they can achieve in one year and under-

estimate what they can achieve in ten years" (I might have mentioned this one before!)

I have to be honest and say that I'm not sure that is entirely true. I think what we, as human beings, can achieve in one year is a phenomenal amount if we put our minds to it, commit to it and take action. We can massively change any part of our lives within one year by committing to the change and then taking action.

Imagine for a moment that you are on a running track, you know, one of the Olympic running tracks that is 400 metres around. You decide that you will take one step forward each and every day for one year and, on average, your step is one metre in length. After one year you have covered 365 metres and completed nearly a whole lap of that track. How far would you have gotten if you had done nothing?

If we transpose that to our lives and commit to taking a minimum of one action per day on a specific area that we want to change, how far could we get? Well, here's the thing..... If you commit to a minimum of one action per day you will move a long way forward in your life. But, there will be days when you can take two, three, four or more actions in a day and instead of just 365 actions you might end up taking 450 or even 500..... How much would that change your life?

All of a sudden you have gone around that running track and then some more, you've covered a massive amount of distance, all by committing to taking a minimum of one action per day for an entire year. Whether it is the weekend or you are on vacation, you still take one action even if it is only small. It may be a public holiday, take an action! You may not feel well, take an action! No matter what is going on, take an action!

I call this my Challenge365 program and I use it because I did it first to try it out and see how far I could get. I chose to focus on my business and create something bigger and better that would help more people than I ever thought possible. For the last year I have taken at least one action every day (and writing this book is part of those actions). Within these 300 or so days (I've not quite finished the year yet!) I have created courses that have helped over 25000 people and rising, more than I thought possible when I started this challenge. I've also started writing this book and it will be finished and released before the year is out.

My business has not only allowed me to help many people but also to spend more time at home with my wife. She has a major spinal injury and, as the years pass by, she needs my help and support more and more. You see, the actions I take every day do not just affect my business, they affect my entire life.

I don't say all of this to impress you, I say it to impress upon you the difference you can make in your own life in just one year. You won't just notice the difference in that one area, the movement appears in many areas of your life even though you just focus on one.

So here it is, I offer you the opportunity to join in my Challenge365...... in fact I hereby challenge you to change one area of your life over the course of the next year and see which other areas of your life benefit from it as well.

Decide, right here and now, which area of your life you are going to focus on and then start taking actions. Start taking actions today so that you start the momentum rolling and then take action(s) every single day.

It will be tough at times and it will be easy at others, no matter what you must keep going.

I promise you this, you will be ASTOUNDED at the difference you can make to your own life in just one year and that difference will benefit you for the rest of your life.

Take Action Every Day!

EVOLUTION POINT NUMBER TWENTY ONE

Start When You Stop Yourself

"The life you want, your entire existence, is available to you on the other side of the fear that currently stops you"

\- *Graham Nicholls*

Start When You Stop Yourself

S——Fear has got a bad rep over the years, it seems that as time goes on fear holds more people back. Are we are more fearsome society than we have ever been? Well, in terms of physical fears from dangers around us, maybe. Does that, however, contribute to the fear we experience in our minds about what might happen when we try to do something new?

Is there something that you have always wanted to do, something you've always wanted to achieve and yet something keeps stopping you, holding you back? What is that something that you want to do or achieve? Think about it clearly now.

Does just thinking about it get the pit of your stomach turning? Maybe thinking about it is fine right up until the point of taking an action and then you talk yourself out of it. When I was younger I would get to the point of action and then something inside would make me feel ill and I would use that as an excuse to stop. That, right there is fear and what it can do to you.

I want to give you another way to look at fear though, I want you to understand that this kind of fear can be overcome by looking at it and hearing it's call in a different way. That kind of fear crops up when we know that what are about to do will benefit us (or others and us) in some way and may just change something in our lives. Our brains have an operating system that is thousands of years old and its default setting is to keep us safe. Yet, from changing our lives into something better we do not need to be kept safe so we need to override the default setting.

Imagine for the moment, the loudest alarm clock you could ever hear. It might be one of those old ringing bell type ones, or maybe it's a more modern buzzer, something that will wake you up and get you jumping out of bed. A wake up alarm like this might make you jump but it is not there to scare you, it is there to stir you into action. This is what fear is, a wake up call to get you going...... Just not in the opposite direction.

Learn to notice the moments when fear is kicking in and you are stopping yourself in some way and use that to kick yourself into gear. Start to recognise those moments, not as fearful moments that stop you in your tracks, but as wake up calls to taking action. The moment you notice it, do something about it! Don't wait, don't wonder, deliver! Take action at that exact time so that you move through and past those feelings as quickly as possible. The quicker you do this and the more often you do this you will start to rewire you response to this stimuli, rewire it to an action taking response.

That is, after all, what fear is. A response pattern that you have built up over the years to a specific set of stimuli. Something happens, fear response kicks in and you don't follow through. Now, by taking action instead of inaction, you are going to break that pattern down and create a new one. Once that new pattern is created you have a whole new life in front of you, one that you can create. Your Life, Your Terms.

Can I ask you a question? Yes, I know, I keep asking you questions don't I..... and I'm going to keep doing it!

Do you know the moments when you stop yourself? Do you know the moments where fear kicks in and you stop yourself right in your own tracks? My bet is that you do know, you know just how it feels and exactly what actions and reactions you have to stop yourself. The fact that you can bring those moments into consciousness gives you the clear opportunity to change them, consciously.

It has to be a conscious choice because your subconscious has been running the fear show for far too long. It's time for the conscious to take over and make better decisions, it's time for the conscious to start hearing that alarm clock and choosing a different path.

Here's my favourite way to look at it....... Every time I now catch myself stopping myself I know that what I'm stopping myself from doing is going to be an awesome addition to my life. So I go and do it, does that make sense?

Everytime I stop myself, I start doing what I was stopping myself from doing.

Start when you stop yourself!!

EVOLUTION POINT NUMBER TWENTY TWO

Know what is important

"Do what you have to do now so that you can do what you want to do later"

\-   *Oprah Winfrey*

K now what is important

Do you know what is important to you? I'm not talking here about paying bills or ensuring there is food on the table for your family (yes, I know those are important things). What I'm talking about is knowing what is important to the core of who you are.

So often I meet people through coaching that are completely unhappy in their lives and just can't figure out why. In that moment I know that they are not living to what they find important and the reason for this is that they do not know what they find important. That may sound like a strange thing to say, how can someone not know what is important to them? How can they not live to what is important to them?

In my life as a Coach / Helping Practitioner, the things we find important are called our Values. They are feelings, emotions and parts of our character that we value. One problem with this is that, very often, those values are set up completely unconsciously when we are young. We tend to pick up similar values to those who are significant in our upbringing, parents, grandparents and our closest friends all have an influence as we mature.

The other problem is that our values change throughout our lives and again this usually happens in our unconscious mind, we know very little about it consciously. Let me give you an example; when you were 18-20 what did you find important in your life? Being an individual maybe? Or maybe finding friends with similar interests? Maybe you enjoyed going out and partying the night away or staying up all night watching movies and having a laugh with your friends.

As you mature these things start to change for most of us. What we do for a living becomes important. When you get married and have children your values change altogether because going out and partying all night is replaced by making sure your family is taken care of. As most people pass 40 years old their health suddenly becomes much more important than it may of been in their earlier years.

The trouble with all of this, as previously stated, is that it all happens in our unconscious mind. Without investigating what we find important we can never live to that, unless it is by chance of course. We end up going about our lives in a way that we think is right, but we don't actually know what is right for us.

Imagine for a moment that one of your top values is health and being healthy on a daily basis and yet you drink too much, smoke and you are consistently eating a poor diet without exercising. Consciously you are ok with your choice but your unconscious is going bonkers trying to tell you that what you are doing is wrong. The unconscious has no direct way of communicating with your conscious so it can't knock on the door and say "excuse me, you are doing this all wrong".

Instead you start to get feelings of frustration or anger, maybe you start to feel upset, sad or down and yet you have no idea why. Now imagine that you are working against more than of your values, maybe two or three of them. How will you feel then? Would you feel unhappy in your life but not know why? You bet!

One of the biggest shifts I ever see people make is when they discover their values and then start to live to them. All of a sudden it is like they realise what their life should be about and they are free. It takes some time to move towards living with their values as there are old patterns that need to be conquered but they now have a conscious understanding and therefore a conscious choice.

So I'll ask you the question again, do you know what is important to you? If you have been through and discovered your values before you are ahead of the crowd and if not then it's time to do so. Discovering your values is a fairly simple process that can take between thirty minutes and an hour. Grab yourself a piece of paper and draw a line down the middle and then answer the following questions:

1 - Over the last three to four months what has been most important to you?

2 - Over your lifetime what has been most important to you?

Your answers will usually be single words and you should write down as many as you need to, it's usual to have anywhere between eight and fifteen. Here's some ideas to get you started (they won't all be applicable to you):

Honesty, Truth, Integrity, Peace, Love, Giving, Contribution, Learning, Growth, Abundance, Authenticity, Acceptance, Health, Patience, Optimism, Honour, Justice, Credibility, Maturity, Decisiveness, Meaning, Purpose.

Once you have this written out you can then decide which of these is most important and which of these is not quite so important (obviously they are all important to you or you wouldn't have written them down). The reason we do this is to discover which ones we need to focus on living to first. So take a look at your list and ask yourself which are the top three, the three most important things to you on that list.

Go on, give it a go now........ I'll wait!

You now know what the most important things are in your life, now comes the difficult question. Focussing on those top three to start with, do you live positively to those three most of the time? In other words, if your top value is love do you give love unconditionally? If one of them is health, do you live a healthy lifestyle? If one is honesty, are you honest or are there times when you bend the truth?

It is often hard at this point because we don't like to criticise ourselves in this way and yet when we do this exercise the path might become clear as to where some of our issues sit. If you live positively to those top three then check through the rest, just to make sure. From this point on you can now decide how you are going to live positively towards the things you find important in life. As mentioned before, it might take some time to break old patterns but it is well worth the effort..... Your life may never be the same again.

I always encourage people to redo their values list every three to four months as things can change swiftly. Things don't change only with age and maturity, they change with major life occurrences - marriage, children, loss of job, death of someone close, major health scare - can all have an effect on what you find important. So remember this exercise and if you truly want to transform your life complete it fully.

Know what is important!

EVOLUTION POINT NUMBER TWENTY THREE

Be Consistently Persistent

"A river cuts through a rock not because of its power, but because of its persistence"

\-   *Anon*

B e Consistently Persistent

There's an old saying that states that the night is darkest just before dawn, in other words when you are struggling the most a breakthrough is coming. The problem with that is most people give up long before dawn breaks. We seem to live in a world where struggle is the enemy, there appears to be a belief that everything should come to us easily. "I should have what I want, how I want it, when I want it and by the way I want it now" is becoming that rallying call of a generation.

The instant gratification market is booming, you can instantly chat with anyone around the world as if they were in the very same room. Films and TV shows are instantly available to watch no matter the time of day or night. You can even order stuff for same day delivery from certain companies so that you don't even have to wait 24 hours for your goods.

The problem with all of this is that people think everything should be on those terms, that success should be instant, money should be instant, a loving and healthy relationship should be instant. It's just not the case!

There is a forgotten universal law that states that anything worth having or doing takes time to work on, build and cultivate. The perfect crop of vegetables does not grow overnight, a child does not grow into an adult within 24 hours and (to coin an old phrase) Rome was not built in a day. Yet when things take time and sometimes show signs of a struggle people run away faster than Warp Speed on the Starship Enterprise (please excuse the Star Trek reference if you are not a fan!).

To get a life that you want, your life on your terms, takes time and effort but more than that it takes consistent persistence. Creating the artwork of any part of your life is a responsibility only you can endure but endure you must..... It is, after all, your life we are talking about.

Life was not designed to be easy, if it was we would be bored. Have you seen the film "The Matrix"? In it one of the main 'baddies' says to Keanu Reeves' character that they had originally built a Matrix where everything was perfect but the human mind couldn't handle it. Our brains were not designed for perfection, they were designed as creative action takers. The bumps, turns, hills, swerves and mountains that we come across in life are all part of the experience.

We are designed to grow and that is what these obstacles are put there for, opportunities for us to grow and be something more. That which does not grow dies; life just wants to make sure that you are always growing but to do that our current society needs to stop giving up so easily. Whoever told us that we could have everything we wanted, when we wanted it basically sold us a lie!

Ok..... I need to stop ranting! My apologies for that coming over as a bit of a rant, it's something I'm particularly passionate about. Why? Well, I've done the same! For many years in my early life I simply didn't like the struggle, I didn't like the fight and I wanted everything to be easy. Of course, life kept trying to tell me that it couldn't be like that and wasn't going to be like that. Did I learn from all of those messages? No, of course I didn't. Instead of using my energy to keep moving forwards through the struggles and hard times I used it to fight back and believe me it takes more energy to fight back that to keep going.

Fortunately, for me, I finally got the message. Something somewhere inside me woke up and gave me a proverbial slap around the face and that is what I want for you (not to slap you around the face!). What I want for you is to realise that, just because you have given up before or just because things are tough or you are struggling..... You don't have to give up this time.

Consistent Persistence wins out in the end. As long as you are working towards something that provides purpose, joy and love in your life you will make it through.

At this point there are usually a bunch of questions that come up:

"How do I know if what I am doing is the right thing for me?"

"How do I know if I am taking the right actions?"

"How do I know if it's working?"

How do I know..... How do I know...... How do I know?

The simple answer is..... You don't! These questions take a step backwards to the instant gratification outlook as people want the results to be proving themselves from step one. Very rarely do you do the first thing and everything else falls into place, it takes much more than one action.

I once heard Dr Wayne Dyer (if you are not sure who he is, google him) tell the story of writing and releasing his most successful book. While he had written books before there was something about this one that he just knew was going to be a smash hit and would help people the world over. However, his publicist wasn't so confident and didn't want to produce too many copies, 1500 were produced to start with with the promise of producing double the amount if they sold.

Dr Dyer actually set himself a business up as a book shop (out of his garage) and bought all 1500 copies of the book just so more were produced. He then got in his car and spent the next few months driving to virtually every state in the USA selling his books to bookstores. To start with the bookstores were not too keen on buying it, but because he wasn't going to give up, he changed his approach. Upon entering a new city he would stop at a payphone, open the directory to bookstores and would ring them asking if they had his book in, of course not telling them he was the author calling! He would call each of them 4 or 5 times, using different accents, asking for this wonderful new book.

Later that day he would then turn up at the bookstores and offer them his book. The store owners, of course, thought they already had interest from customers so snapped up a few copies. But he still didn't stop there as he knew that to continue selling books the bookstore owners had to actually sell them. He therefore visited the local radio stations, who were crying out for content, and talked about his new book live on air.

People heard these interviews and promptly went and bought his book from the bookstores who then had to contact the publisher to order more. He spent months circling the country, calling bookstores and pretending to be customers who wanted to buy the book, then visiting the bookstores and selling them his book and finally being interviewed on radio stations.

What happened? His book became a New York Times Best Seller and stayed at the top of the charts for many weeks. It has been translated into many languages and sold millions of copies all over the world. The book is called "Your Erroneous Zones"

Did Dr Dyer show Consistent Persistence? You bet he did! He didn't give up when the publicist only wanted to produce 1500, he changed his strategy when bookstores weren't buying from him and he made sure the book would be sold by being interviewed on as many radio stations as he could get on. Without him doing all of that his book may have never found its way past the first 1500 copies!

When have you given up too easily that, if you had followed through, it would change your life?

When have you let issues and struggles get the better of you and decided not to carry on?

If you were honest with yourself right here and right now, what should you have carried on with that would help shape your life on your terms?

GREAT NEWS!

Just because you have stopped in the past doesn't mean you can't start again and follow through this time. Yesterday has gone, the future is not here yet and right here and now is a gift.... That's why it's called the present!

You have the opportunity right here and now to start your consistent persistence approach to creating your life on your terms. You can state right here and now that you are going to do whatever it takes to make this life yours and you are going to do it consistently with persistence until it is done.

Will you commit to that right here and now?

Go on.......

Be Consistently Persistent!

EVOLUTION POINT NUMBER TWENTY FOUR

See Opposites of the Norm

"Sane is the insanity most call normality put forth by society"

\-   *Erik Till*

See Opposites of the Norm

See Opposites of the Norm
Every big invention, every shift in thinking, every major move in society and every life changing creation was the result of thinking outside of the norm. Doing and trying something that had never been done and, in most cases, was outside

of what most people would call conventional.

Lives don't change by following the 'normal' path. In fact, by the very definition, lives that follow the normal path are...... well .... Normal! You don't want that for your life, I know that because you are reading this book and you have got this far in. Some people will have run back to normality by now, they will be settling for their normal life. That's ok, by the way, if that is their choice. You, on the other hand, want something different and that takes something different.

From an early age, we are told by our parents and teachers how life is supposed to be and, of course, as impressionable young minds we take that in and believe it to be true. It is only when we grow and mature do some of us start to question those norms and wonder "what if". To truly transform your life you must not think the way you have thought up until this very point, you must think in opposition to the norm. It is only in that space of un-normality (not sure if that's actually a word in the English dictionary but maybe it should be) that freedom of thought comes.

At some point in the not to distant past, someone thought outside of the norm about a job. They decided that they didn't want to get up each day and go in to work, so they thought in opposition to the norm. They found a way to work from home with the internet being key to that shift. But that wasn't enough for some as they didn't want to be trapped in their house all day so a new way of living emerged and a new phrase was adopted - Digital Nomad!

A Digital Nomad is someone who travels the world consistently while running (usually) an internet based business. They log on using free wifi hotspots in any city, do their work and then carry on travelling. Can you imagine trying to explain what a digital nomad is to someone from the 1950's or 1960's? It is the exact opposite of what the 'norm' was in that era.

If someone hadn't thought in opposition to the norm we may still be riding on horseback to get everywhere rather than using cars, buses, trains or planes. If someone hadn't thought in opposition to the norm, the only way to talk face-to-face with someone on the other side of the world would be to go and visit them. Now we have video calling that connects in milliseconds and is perfect clarity. If someone hadn't thought in opposition to the norm, the only way you would have read this book would be to go to a bookstore and buy a copy printed on paper. You may be reading this on a digital device right now, or you may be reading a paper copy but it wasn't bought from a bookstore. In fact, this book may never have got published unless someone came up with self-publishing!!

Do I need to go on?

Now, I'm not suggesting that you have to invent the next world changing creation or the next humanity shifting technology. What I am suggesting is that, to transform your life, you need to stop thinking in the normal ways you have been doing and make a shift to thinking in opposition to it. It's worth pointing out that what is normal to you may not be normal to me or to anyone else on this planet. You have your own normality and it is your normality that needs challenging in order to transform your life.

An individual life is changed ONLY by thinking differently. Everything we do or create is first created by our thoughts, in our minds. Take a look around you and know that everything you see was once a thought in someone's mind. This book was a product of my mind, the device you are reading it on was created in someone's mind, the cup you drink your coffee out of in the morning was created....... In someone's mind.

Your life, as it stands now, was created in your mind and by your choices and decisions which occured...... ok, you get the picture! Remember right back at the start of the book when we spoke about responsibility? From here on out, the responsibility for creating your life on your terms relies solely on you and your ability to think in opposition to what has become your normality.

If you don't like your normal job....... Think un-normally!

If you don't like the normal house you are living in....... Think un-normally!

If you don't like your normal relationship...... Think un-normally!

If you don't like any normal situation in your life...... Think un-normally!

While you continue to think in normal terms you will continue on with your current normal life. You bought and picked up this book because you were after something different in your life and that something is un-normality!

I could have carried on in my normal job but it bored me to tears and I wanted something more so I started Coaching. But it wasn't enough when I first started to sustain me so I started my own business as a consultant which meant I had more control over my work. Then I met my wife who has a major spinal injury (I think I've mentioned that already) and as time went on I knew I needed to support her by being home more. I found a website that sold online video courses that I could create and sell on and, although I'd never done anything like that before, I decided to go for it. It was so far outside my norm it really was in complete opposition.

Now, I work from home so that I can be here to support my wife, I create courses that are sold all over the world and I'm sitting here writing this book for you to read. If anyone had told me fifteen years ago that I would be doing this I would have laughed and told them "Nah, that's not me..... I'm too normal for that"

Transform your life.

See Opposites of the Norm!

EVOLUTION POINT NUMBER TWENTY FIVE

Know the truth about Thoughts and Emotions

"Healing comes from taking responsibility; to realise that it is you - and no one else - that creates your thoughts, your feelings and your actions"

\- *Peter Shepherd*

Know the truth about Thoughts and Emotions

Know the truth about Thoughts and Emotions Two of the biggest lies in the history of humankind reside in the area of thoughts and emotions. I use the word 'lies' reservedly because it's not like people are concealing this information; it's just not as widespread as it needs to be. Here are the two truths that you need to know in order to transform your life:

1) Thoughts are not real, they are merely thoughts that can be accepted or ignored

2) Emotions are within your control, they do not control you

We believe and are led to believe that our thoughts and emotions control us, they control our lives and determine who we are and who we are going to be. Nothing could be further from the truth.

Let's take thoughts as a starting point.....

The moment a human being, like your good self, opens their mind and discovers that thoughts are not real..... Change happens. A shift occurs and a realisation takes place that you don't need to listen to everything that pops into your head and in that moment you are freed. You are freed from the belief that you are tied to each and every thought that appears from nowhere. You are, all of a sudden, given a choice of whether to engage those thoughts or discard them, wipe them away and tell them to go 'do one'!

Let's be honest here for a second, we all have thoughts that we could wonder **"where the hell did *that* come from?"** don't we. It's like a balloon popping and thousands of bits of confetti are thrown into the air, each one containing a different thought and most of them random at best.

Nobody can ever really agree as to where thoughts come from in the first place. If you talk to a scientist they may well tell you that it is merely the electrons in your brain firing and BOOM..... There's a thought. Psychologists and Psychotherapists may tell you that they come from the unconscious mind as it throws up weird things and memories all in an effort to do what it believes is right for us. Someone with more spiritual traits might put it down to a higher power or the universe and those with a religious persuasion may invoke the name of their particular religious figure.

Do you know something, to me it doesn't matter where they come from particularly. What matters is that thoughts crop up, pop into your mind like popping candy and that not one of them is true until you make it come true. The way you make it come true is to grab hold of it, buy into it and use it...... how often though, have you done that and it's turned out to be complete hogwash?

I've met people who had the thought that their partner was cheating on them, they grabbed hold of that thought and ran with it. They confronted their partner and called them a cheat only for their partner to not only refute but also prove otherwise. At that point though, trust was broken and the relationship died away.

A common thought that hurts people because they grab it and believe in it is that they are not enough or not good enough, we discussed this earlier in the book didn't we. People all over the world don't live the life they want to because they have bought into the thought that they are not good enough to change. They don't even try to live their life on their terms because of that one simple little thought, it is paralysing to them.

For far too many years we have allowed these thoughts to rule the roost, allowing them to control our actions and behaviours. It's time for a change..... In fact, it's not just time for a change it is a necessity for change. Those thoughts are always going to appear but when you take control you decide if they carry any weight and you do that by seeking the truth.

If you have a consistent thought that is holding you back or paralysing you, stopping your progress towards the life you want start to ask yourself......

Is that really true?

What is the real truth in this situation?

Ask over and over again and go on a hunt for the truth, as the old saying goes *"the truth will set you free"* Be 100% honest with yourself, don't just accept the bull that those thoughts are selling, dig deep down and make a rational, truth based choice. Challenge each thought that holds you back or means you harm and eradicate it. It may show up in a different format and all you do is cut it down over and over again.
The shift to awareness that your thoughts don't control you, you control them is HUGE in your life and is essential for any transformation you wish to make. Your thoughts will try to stop you, don't try to fight them back, break them down with the truth.

Now what about those pesky Emotions?

Much like thoughts, we have been led to understand that our emotions are uncontrollable and, in fact, control us. We accept, with far too much ease, that a bad mood overtakes us and does not allow us to do anything about it. We allow sadness, frustration, depression and anxiety to control our lives when, truth be known, they are emotions that can be worked on and controlled.

I am in full awareness that this part of our conversation may disturb some of you and you may even consider closing the book and never picking it up again. It is tough to learn that the way we have let our emotions rule us all our lives was in error and we could have done something about it. But I urge you to stick with me here as we run through this section of the book, it may just open your life up to what you want it to be.

In Cognitive Behavioural Therapy (CBT) we call it 'flooding' when an emotion completely takes over us and it is very true that our emotional reactions happen much quicker than our thought reactions. Yet our thought reactions catch up pretty quickly. We might react with anger or rage to a certain situation but we do not need to carry that on. Using a tool from CBT called the STOP BUTTON we can halt that emotional response before it does any damage. The STOP BUTTON is exactly what it sounds like, we train our mind to shout STOP in reaction to an emotional response.

This halts the initial response and we can then examine whether it is an appropriate course of action. It is a skill that is built through repetition (like all good skills) that benefits us as we control what may have previously been uncontrollable.

More than this though, we can dissect an emotion into its parts so that we know how to cut the power to each part like cutting the electricity between a light switch and bulb. You'll remember, earlier in the book, we talked about "Love Rules", well each emotion has rules to it. Those certain things that have to happen for you to feel that emotion. Try it for a moment, instead of thinking of your love rules as we did earlier, think about you "joy' rules. What has to happen for you to feel joyful? List them out just like before and you'll have your joy rules and once you have them you could consciously change them if you want to.

We can, though, go deeper into emotion than that to really learn how to cut their power and diminish the light of the emotions we do not want to feel as often. This I call the PALM Framework for Emotions. If you put your hand up in front of you (it doesn't matter which one) you can imagine the word PALM spelled out under each of your four fingers (not the thumb). Your Index finger has the letter P at its base, your Middle Finger has the A seated there, your Ring Finger houses the letter L and then, finally you Little Finger possesses the M. Each of these four letters make up the framework of an emotion and with that framework we can discover how emotions happen to you and how you can change them.

Let's take a look at them individually:

P = Physical Association.

Each emotional state will have a particular physical association for you, if I asked you to act out being happy or joyful what would you do? You would maybe smile, your eyes would widen, your shoulders may drop a little as you relax in the joyful state. You would probably feel an energy running through you and you may choose to jump around, sing or dance. Consider them for a moment, what do you do physically when you feel joyful?

Now consider what you do physically when you get angry, frustrated, down, depressed or anxious. Each has its own unique physical association and recognising it is the first step to changing it.

A = Attention

There's an old saying that states "where focus goes, energy flows" - where you place your attention is how you feel. Let's take love as the example this time shall we? When you feel completely and utterly loved what do you pay attention to? What or who do you think about? Do you think about the good times that you have, or have had, with a loved one or do you focus on everything that is horrible in your life? Of course, you focus on the good times, you attention shifts to suit the emotion in question.

Where does your attention shift to if you're feeling a more negative emotion? Does it focus on the good things in life or all the bad, negative things that have happened or that could happen? Hmmmmm, there's a pattern forming here isn't there.

L = Language

How we use language, either out loud or to ourselves, has a massive effect on how we feel. In fact two men by the name of John Grinder and Richard Bandler spent years studying language and developed Neuro-Linguistic Programming (NLP), a study of how our brains use language and the effects it has. More specific than just language, our emotions are connected to the questions we ask ourselves. When we ask positive and empowering questions we get positive and empowering answers and I'm certain you can figure out that the opposite is also true.

Which is the more empowering question:

1) Why does this always happen to me?

Or

2) How can I stop this happening to me and live a better life?

Clearly number 2 holds the greater power. What sort of questions do you ask yourself on a daily basis..... Empowering or disempowering? Positive or negative?

M = Meaning

As Human Beings we are meaning making machines, we just love to attach a meaning to anything and everything. If there's a situation, an occurrence or an experience we are going to attach a meaning to it. Much like with the questions above though, if we attach a negative, disempowering meaning to a situation we stir up a negative and disempowering emotion. Decide to attach a positive meaning and the emotional response changes in an instant.

The truth is that any situation can hold any meaning we want it to because we decide. A meaning is nothing more than a thought that we grab hold of and as you have discovered already, thoughts are not real. A simple question to ask to help with this is:

What else could this mean?

Come up with as many answers as you can and you have the opportunity to choose a meaning that works for you.

You can now go through each of your emotional states, particularly the ones you want to feel less of and understand their framework, their make-up if you will. By doing that you give yourself the option to break each of the steps of that framework down. The Physical Association can be broken by doing something radically different (consider going for a walk or run, maybe dancing and singing along to music). You can place your attention, consciously, on a different and more appropriate area of your life. Training yourself to ask better questions takes some work but is worth every moment you spend doing it and empowering questions often start with the word 'How'. Finally, I have already given you the answer of how to change the meaning you attach to something. Discover as many meanings as you can and choose an appropriate one.

With this framework and these steps you take control of your emotional state. Will you still feel sad, upset, angry or frustrated in the future? Yes, but you now don't have to live in that state, you can change it and take control of your life.

This has been a heavy chapter but a worthwhile one and I hope that you now understand that your thoughts and emotions do not control you..... You control them!

Know the truth about Thoughts and Emotions!

EVOLUTION POINT NUMBER TWENTY SIX

Learn the Joy of Tapping

"Once your negative emotions, beliefs, and experiences have been processed and released, you're free to feel and be positive again"

\- *Nick Ortner*

Learn the Joy of Tapping

LIf you had asked me, a few years ago, the best way to work through and release negative emotions, feelings, thoughts and beliefs I would have taken you through a Life Coaching or NLP (Neuro-Linguistic Programming) process. I would have asked you a series of questions designed to stimulate different thoughts and processes in search of the truth because, ultimately, the truth *will* set you free.

108 | LIFE EVOLUTION

Since then, however, I have discovered something called 'tapping' and I am going to actively encourage you to do the same as it is mind-bendingly easy to use and powerful in seeing you through tough emotions, thoughts and beliefs. If you are interested in learning then I have a couple of courses that you can learn from, check out the *'Additional Resources'* section at the end of the book!

Tapping is based on the Meridian Energy System within the body, the same system that acupuncture uses so effectively to help with many ailments. However, instead of sticking needles into the body you can learn to simply tap on certain points in a certain order and, combined with language and focus, this tapping can help release those negative thoughts and emotions.

Tapping started with Dr Roger Callahan who took the eastern practices of acupuncture and acupressure and developed a process he called "Thought Field Therapy" or TFT for short. One of his students, Gary Craig, took what Dr Callahan was teaching, changed little parts of it, expanded on it and created a system he called Emotional Freedom Techniques or EFT for short. Both of these processes are powerful in their own right, which is why I teach both of them in my courses. For the purposes of this section of the book though I am going to encourage you to learn and understand the EFT process.

While Dr Callahan developed different tapping routines (or Algorithms as he called them) for different ailments, Gary Craig turned EFT into a 'one-stop-shop' process that could help with many things using just one routine (or recipe in EFT terms). It's worth pointing out at this point that, as with many things, EFT has been changed and developed over the years as others have taken it on and put their own spin on it. If you have a search on YouTube you will find Gary Craig's work alongside many others who do it their own way.

These differing ways should not deflect from the fact that Tapping, in any form, is a powerful medium in which to help yourself. Whether you want to help yourself to overcome anxiety, depression, stress, grief or trauma, whether you want to help yourself with physical pain relief (both short term and chronic), whether you want to move past fear and limiting beliefs or phobias, Tapping can help. There are even books and courses out there that use Tapping to help with weight loss and self confidence…. The list is endless.

Let's run through the basics of tapping shall we, so that you can start to use it and feel the benefits of it. Depending on whether you work with TFT or EFT will determine whether you say something out loud about the problem you are working on whilst tapping or you focus internally on a specific issue. For the purposes of this chapter I'm going to suggest that you simply focus inwardly on the issue you want to release and as you tap on each point you can start to feel it slip away and release you from it's grip.

Before beginning any Tapping with my clients I always start with some deep breathing so that they can relax into the process. Therefore, I'm going to suggest that you do the same. Once you have read through where the Tapping points are, go through a deep breathing exercise for just two to three minutes before starting.

Here are the Tapping points and how to find them:

- The Karate Chop Point - the point on the side of the hand that you might normally associate with a Karate Chop. Halfway between the knuckle for the little finger and the wrist. We always start with this point and it is the only point we tap on for 25 to 30 taps.
- The Top of the Head - Halfway between the crown of the head and the hairline on your forehead.
- The Corner of the Eyebrow - This is the corner of the eyebrow nearest the nose.

- The Corner of the Eye - The very outside corner of the eye, right on the edge of the bony part of the eye socket.
- Under the Eye - Again, right on the edge of the bony part of the eye socket, in the middle of the width of the eye.
- The Upper Lip - Halfway between the bottom of the nose and the top lip, right in the middle of the width of the mouth.
- The Chin - Halfway between the bottom lip and the bottom of the chin, right in the middle of the width of the mouth
- The Collarbone - Following the collarbone (either side) inwards until it stops just below the throat. There is a small dip between the two collarbones, right on the edge of either side is this tapping point
- Under the Arm - For the ladies out there, this is roughly where you bra strap sits underneath your armpit. For the gentlemen, imagine a point about a handwidth, or just over, down from your armpit.
- Thumb and Fingers - The very bottom of the thumbnail / fingernail where the corner of the U is, each side of that U can be tapped. Following in from the thumb, index finger, middle finger, ring finger and finally the little finger.
- Return to the Karate Chop Point.

The basic process works like this, consider for a moment an emotion that you want to feel less of..... an emotion that would improve your life if you had relief from it. Keep that in your mind as you, firstly breath nice and deeply for two to three minutes. Breathing in and out nice and deeply, not forced, just deeper than you would normally breath.

Once you have gone through this deep breathing for two or three minutes start to tap on the points in the order described above. Tapping around 25-30 times on the Karate Chop Point to start with and then 7 to 10 times on each of the other points in order. Finally returning to the Karate Chop Point for another 25 to 30 taps. This whole tapping process can then be repeated for two or three cycles.

What tapping on each of these points is doing is releasing the energy of each key point in the Meridian System. Dr Callahan postulated that the 'blocks' in energy at each or any of these points would be party to creating the negative emotional states. Releasing these blocks allows us to deal with, and get past, those negative emotional states and releasing us to enjoy more of our lives.

Does this work first time? For some people, yes it does, for others it takes more time. But I prefer to see the further reaching benefits of tapping and understand it as not just a quick solution to a specific problem, but as an ongoing process of improving my life.

While I help clients with the aid of Tapping I will always encourage them to make it part of a daily routine. For me Tapping is more than just a 'deal with an issue' routine, it helps me to relax and focus on the day, it helps me be in the present moment and it helps me understand the power of mind and body in combination.

Why would you wait until your energy system is blocked in some way and then start tapping, only to stop again once you feel a bit better? Tapping has no negative effects and can be used at any time and should be used all of the time. In my humble opinion, it is better to keep the energy pathways clear through consistent daily use of Tapping rather than waiting until something happens. Having my energy systems flowing in full effect is critical to my life and my work so I have a daily practice of using Tapping to benefit myself and the people who I have the honour of helping.

Just before we move on, I sometimes get asked how people with neck and arm injuries can use Tapping if they are unable to tap because of their limited movement. As I have researched Tapping more and more I have discovered that the mind - body connection is ultimately powerful in its oneness. To the point that we don't actually need to tap on each point individually, we can place our focus on each point for a short while and have the same effect as Tapping on each point.

Remember the exercise where I had you close your eyes and feel your pulse somewhere in your body? Use that level of attention and focus on each point for ten to fifteen seconds each and the Karate Chop point for thirty to forty seconds. Breathe first, just like you did before and then focus on each point in turn..... You may be surprised by the outcomes.

Whichever way you decide to do it, make sure that you Learn the Joy of Tapping!

EVOLUTION POINT NUMBER TWENTY SEVEN

Understand What Purpose Is

"It doesn't interest me what you do for a living. I want to know what you ache for, and if you dream of meeting your heart's longing"

\- *Oriah*

Understand What Purpose Is

You'll notice, I'm certain, that I didn't call this section *"Understand What YOUR Purpose is"* and I have done that for a reason. Before understanding your purpose you need to understand what purpose actually is. There are many books, audio's, seminars, coaches and so-called guru's out there that will claim that they can help you find your '*true purpose*' and the '*thing you were meant to do*' and yet, for me, they miss the point of what purpose really is.

Purpose IS NOT something you do! Let me say that again...... Purpose IS NOT something you do!

We seem to have been tricked into the way of thinking that to find our purpose, we must be doing one specific thing with our lives. We are told that to find our purpose, we must get the job or career that calls to us most or be chasing a dream that wakes us up and makes us jump out of bed every morning with passion and desire. Many tell us that finding our purpose is about taking actions that create a difference in the world.

For me though, purpose is much simpler than that. It is not about taking action, it is not about getting the job or career that calls to us and it is not about chasing a dream. Those may be a part of it but at it's very core, at the heart of it all, our Purpose is a feeling within our hearts that says we are living our lives on our terms. That's right.... Purpose is a feeling and not an action or a thing..... A feeling.

When we see our Purpose as an action or a thing we tend to assume that it has to be this HUGE action or this HUGE thing that we have to have or do. We instantly put pressure on ourselves by thinking that our Purpose needs to be world changing, life defining and gargantuan in nature. Is it any wonder that people struggle to find their Purpose? We scare ourselves out of it before we can even think about it!

There is a difference between Purpose and Reason and that is where the confusion resides. Our Reason to be here, in this life and on this planet may well be an action or a thing and yet it doesn't have to be the HUGE thing that we associate with Purpose. Is there any greater Reason to be here than to provide for our family? I think not! What about helping another Human Being....... If your Reason in life was to help just one Human Being a day, whether it be helping an old lady across the street or a mother struggling to lift her baby's pushchair onto a bus, would that be a good Reason to be here? Again, I think so. You may decide that your Reason is to contribute to society and help as many people as you can across your lifetime which is a bigger Reason for sure, but not unattainable.

But...... be certain that your Reason DOES NOT define your Purpose. The actions you take and the things that you do or have does not define who you are and the Purpose you feel in your heart. What I mean by that is that you do not have to have a Reason that is world changing, your Reason should be in line with who you are. The actions you take every day and the things you do should align with you..... The you at your very core!

People seem to want to try and push open the door to Purpose and yet every single door that leads to our Purpose opens inwards. Only when we learn to open those doors inwards and go within ourselves do we discover that our Purpose is inside, our Purpose is at the very core of our being. When we do that and discover the Purpose within our Reasons become clear.

Imagine for a moment, if you will, that every action you take and everything that you do was to fulfil that feeling inside, that feeling of Purpose. No matter what day, week, month or year it was, no matter what time of day nor how you felt, you would still fulfil your Purpose by fulfilling your life. How would it feel to know that your Purpose is not something you find to do but, instead is something that is already inside you just waiting to be discovered?

It cannot be discovered in the physical world, it cannot be found in the taking of actions or owning of things. It can only be found by taking the journey inside to the place where your true self resides. It is that place that was created inside you long before you were born, it was hard-wired into every fibre of your being, your soul, your spirit and your heart. This is where Purpose is found for this is where Purpose always has been and will always be...... waiting for you to find it.

To discover your Purpose first you need to Understand What Purpose Is!

(Now that you know...... go in search my friend, go inside)

EVOLUTION POINT NUMBER TWENTY EIGHT

Know Thyself....... Be Thyself

"Do thine own work, and know thyself"

\- *Plato*

K now Thyself........ Be Thyself

Within a couple of the sections we have gone through in this book so far I have talked about how important the true you is. That being inside who sits at your very core, the one you were born to be. You know, the Creative one, the Purposeful one, the Loving one, the one who works from pure joy.

Much like with discovering our Purpose, many people around the world struggle to find themselves. They live their lives in search of something that will never be found on the outside and will never be found in what we do. We are not *'Human Doings'* we are *'Human Beings'* and to discover our true self we must "be" rather than "do".

One of our greatest drivers in life is to consistently be who we believe we are and yet most people believe themselves to be actions, reactions, emotions or behaviours and we are none of them. Have you ever known someone who identifies as lazy? Or how about someone who identifies as a smoker? It becomes who they believe they are and that is a powerful draw.

Let's do a simple exercise that is designed to help you start to uncover your true self. Get a fresh piece of paper and draw two columns, one that has "*I am.......*" at the top and one that has "*I am a.......*" at the top.

The question to ask yourself is........ Who am I? And then fill out the columns with answers that are one and two words at most. Don't expect everything to come all at once, it sometimes takes time to really work through who you really are so you may keep getting answers over the next few days.

A couple of things to remember:

- You are not behaviours (Lazy, Smoker etc.)
- You are not an emotion or emotional reaction (Angry, Frustrated, Depressed, Anxious)
- You are not your job
- You are you. You are your Values, your Purpose and you are what is in your heart.

Let's see how you get on.......
How did you get on? I hope you followed through and com-

pleted the exercise, even if you have done it before it is always worth working through it again to reaffirm your previous thoughts.

Take the time to look over your answers and understand that this is the starting of who you are at your core. I say it is the starting of who you are because there is much more to you than this, these are just your conscious answers. You have started a process now where your unconscious will also work on the question of who are you? Be wary of its answers and as they come, take time to consider them and decide whether they fit with you and who you now believe you are.

The next step is to combine these answers with the Values that we discovered earlier in the book and you start to get an insight into who you really are. Then, just like with the Values, you have a choice of whether to live as that person or not. Living to the person you are in your core means living an authentic life and it is truly liberating. The freedom of mind and spirit that you feel when you live with authenticity is astounding as not many people have the understanding to do so.

To **know thyself** is a great step forward in life and to **be thyself** is ultimate freedom.

Once you start to be thyself you understand that you are much more than those words on a page, much more than your emotions and far more than your values. You, the truest, purest you is more than the body that you inhabit, you are a soul and spirit that loves to be free. Living with the freedom of self allows you to understand just how connected you are, not only connected to yourself but connected to everything and everyone around you.

The entire world, the entire universe looks, sounds and feels different. Being you has the ultimate capacity to connect you with everything and unconnect you from everything all at the same time.

Ok, ok, I know I'm going deep here and the reason is that I want you to know just how far you can reach.

The power is not just in Knowing Thyself, to Be Thyself is freedom!

EVOLUTION POINT NUMBER TWENTY NINE

Understand that Reality is Yours Alone

"Death is not the greatest loss in life. The greatest loss is what dies inside us while we live"

- *Norman Cousins*

U nderstand that Reality is Yours Alone

The great thing about discovering who you are at your core (see last chapter) is that you start to understand reality in a different way.

"He's just not living in the real world"

"She needs a reality check"

"What they are saying is just not the reality of the situation"

Have you heard any or all of those phrases before? I suspect you have, or at least something similar to that. There is this huge misconception that reality is real (read that again) and it's not. We have been led to believe that there is only one reality and that it is a constant for everyone. This could not be further from the truth!

Each of us, every individual on the planet has our own reality and it differs from everyone elses. I might even go so far as to say that there is no singular reality that we could ever get to because everything around us relies on our experiences and our consciousness to exist in our reality.

When you look at a beautiful red rose do you see the same rose as I would? How can you know? I may see it from a different angle, I may see a different shade of red as my eyes differ from yours, I may be colourblind and not see it at all like you do, I may have no interest in flowers so pay it no attention. Your 'reality' of that rose is defined by the words you use and mine by my words. You may consider it beautiful, I may consider it ugly. You may consider it red, I may see it as maroon. You see it as a rose while I just see another flower. (Ok, so I love beautiful red roses too..... I'm just making the point).

If you expand this example to everything in life you start to understand the magnitude of what we flippantly call reality. Let's start with life experiences. Can twins, who are born moments apart and have the same parents with apparently the same upbringing turn out to be very different people? Yes, of course they can. They may have had a similar upbringing but they have their consciousness and therefore experience things differently.

No matter how much parents may try to bring them up the same and give them the same education and the same opportunities, they will always be different individuals with different consciousness. This becomes more apparent when they get to school age, while one teacher may engage one of the twins with a particular subject, the other may be bored with it. One loves to read and learn while the other loves to learn through doing things.

If twins, who have apparently had the same upbringing as each other can have such different lives and therefore different realities..... How can we expect that any other two individuals can see reality in the same way? How can we expect that there is one single reality that is constant for everyone? We can't. We all have different experiences and we all see the same situation in different ways and that is what creates our reality.

Let's imagine for a moment that you, I and twenty other people go to a concert. We go to see a band who perform for sixty minutes and afterwards we are all interviewed and asked what the concert was like. Will we all describe it in exactly the same way? Heck no! There will be twenty two different versions of what the concert was like. Some will say it was too loud, some not loud enough. Some will have loved the lights while some hate all the flashing. The lead singers voice was amazing to a few while others thought he was off key.

Did the band play twenty two different concerts all at the same time? No, there were just twenty two different experiences because of the twenty two different consciousnesses.

If it wasn't for consciousness there would be no reality. Our consciousness takes in every experience we have through our senses, it compares it in an instant to our previous experiences, our beliefs and our values and then creates our own version of reality based on that. This makes one thing true, your reality is yours alone and everyone else has their own version.

At the point of writing this there are estimated to be 7.7 Billion people on this amazing planet that we inhabit. That's 7.7 Billion consciousnesses and therefore 7.7 Billion versions of reality. Is reality real? Only to the individual who holds on to it.

What does this mean for us as individuals?

The awesome news is that we create our own reality! We can choose whether the rose is red and beautiful and to stop and admire it or whether to walk by without giving it a second thought. We can choose whether a situation is a problem or something to learn and grow from. We can choose what the reality of success looks like, sounds like and feels like to us rather than what others would have us believe that success is. We get to choose our version of reality.

It also means that everyone else in the world gets to choose their version of reality and that we need to understand that nobody will see, hear and feel everything in the way that we do. It is within our power to accept that we are individuals and that, just because we may not like what others say or do does not make them right or wrong.

Our own version of reality also means that we do not have to live to anyone elses standard or try to live someone else's life. Far too many people try to live the way they think their parents want them to or the way they think their friends will like. Do you know anyone who is in a job they hate simply because it was expected of them by their parents? Or how about anyone who has done some really stupid because their friends were doing it and even though they knew it was wrong they went along with it to please others?

I'll hold my hands up right here and now, in my formative years I was what is known as a pleaser. I would do anything to please others, to make them happy in the hope of fitting in. I even remember thinking to myself that I would do anything to make my family and friends happy even if it was to the detriment of my own happiness and wellbeing. Was I living my life within my reality? No! I was trying to live in everyone else's..... Is it any wonder I suffered with depression, stress and anxiety?

There will always be people who try to push their version of reality on to you because they are under the misguided idea that their reality is real. They have been led to believe, and continue to believe, that there is only one reality..... Theirs. You have a choice to say no, that's not my reality. Is it hard when it's someone close to you who you love and care for? Yes, it is but it is required for your wellbeing and your wholebeing (you remember us talking about your wholebeing right?).

Is reality real? Well, you may think that the chair you are sitting on is solid or that the cushion you are leaning on is soft. If you speak to a physicist, however, they will tell you that solid, hard or soft are only determined by how fast the particles are moving within that certain object...... they have another different form of reality!

Is reality real? If you look at a glass of water in front of you then close your eyes and picture it do you see it as exactly the same? Now when you open your eyes you find that someone has removed it and you are staring at an empty table can you still see it when you close your eyes? You probably can. So was it real or did your consciousness make it real? Did your consciousness decide that it was glass and that it was water? If you tasted the 'water' and it turned out to be something like vodka how quickly would your reality change?

Am I going to far?

The key thing here is to know that your reality is yours and yours alone and that everyone else has their own version. You create your reality with your consciousness, you choose. You cannot affect anyone else's and nobody can affect yours..... Reality is an individual understanding.

What does all this mean? It means that this is your life and your reality and you hold the responsibility to create it in the way you choose....... And the only choice that matters is yours!

Understand that Reality is Yours Alone!

EVOLUTION POINT NUMBER THIRTY

Always Seek Three Perspectives

"When you change the way you look at things,the things you look at change."

- *Dr. Wayne Dyer*

Always Seek Three Perspectives

Always Seek Three Perspectives

The human mind is a phenomenal piece of kit, it has the power to take us anywhere we want to go. We can close our eyes and be somewhere we once visited and see it with absolute clarity, we can hear what was happening at that moment and feel those emotions again. More than that it can create things that we have never seen, heard or felt with that same clarity and make them so vivid that we can believe that they are real.

Actually, when we create something so vividly in our mind, our brain cannot distinguish them as not being real. To our brain it is real in that moment...... another form of reality maybe?

This gives rise to a power, a superpower if you will, that we hold within us..... The power to choose how we want to experience something which carries on nicely from our discussion on reality! We have the ability to see any situation from any number of perspectives in our minds eye. We can literally pick ourselves up and place ourselves at any other place in time and space, then see, hear and feel a situation from that point of view.

That's a superpower right there ladies and gentlemen!

Let's try a little exercise.........

Take yourself back to a conversation you have recently had, it doesn't matter who it was with, or even if you were face to face..... You could have been at the other end of a telephone. After you have read the instructions, close your eyes and follow along.

You can imagine yourself in that conversation right now, being you, saying what you said and hearing what you heard. Be there in that moment and allow yourself to just be you as if you were seeing through your own eyes and hearing through your own ears at that moment.

As the conversation continues allow yourself to just carry on and then feel yourself lift up out of yourself and float away to a short distance away, maybe five to ten metres. Now you can see yourself talking, you are seeing yourself as if you were on a screen and you can hear the words you are saying but they are coming from over where you see yourself. Allow yourself a few moments to listen to the conversation from this observers point of view and notice that you don't feel the emotions from here, you only hear the words and see the video playing in front of you.

Finally, take yourself towards the other person in this conversation. Whether they are across from you or on the other end of the phone, it doesn't matter. Place yourself in their position and hear your voice talking to you, you in their place. What do you see? How differently do you hear the conversation from here? What does it feel like from their perspective? Wait a few moments and take it all in.

Now, bring yourself back to the here and now, open your eyes and reacquaint yourself with the place you are in. Take the time to notice the things around you so that you are fully back in this moment.

Just sit for a few moments and reflect on that experience, reflect on being you reliving the conversation. Was it different this time around? How about reflecting on you as the observer of the conversation, just looking and listening but not feeling anything.... Simply observing, how did that feel? What about placing yourself in the other person's shoes for a short while, what did you think of how you were communicating to them? How was it different from your own perspective?

Now imagine, for just a moment, any other situation recently where something didn't go right or something felt negative. How would you look at this from the observer's perspective? When you are just the observer with no emotional attachment does the situation seem different to you? How could you react differently?

What about a conversation that didn't go well, how would you feel about it if you took the other person's perspective? What would you hear differently? Would you understand their reaction more?

In these moments we can take many perspectives and create many different versions of the event. Different perspectives give us different options when it comes to how we act and react. Options and choices are the things that give us power over our emotions and behaviours. Options and choices are what give us the freedom to be human, the freedom to be ourselves.

The three perspectives you have experienced gives us a wide range of options in a potentially volatile situation. Maybe you are arguing with your spouse and instead of continuing the argument you decide to see it entirely from their point of view, or you take the observer's perspective and remove all emotions from the situation. In that moment you have the power to end the argument instantly and reach a mature conclusion.

What other perspectives could you take? The list is endless......

- Your spouse's
- The observer's
- Your best friend's
- Your parent's
- A stranger's
- Someone you admire
- Your favourite film star
- Your favourite film character
- A role model's
- A mentor's
- The Universes? Why not!

All you have to do is focus and ask yourself *"How would (enter name here) see and hear this, how would they feel about it?"* and listen to the answers.

Just think, if every uncomfortable situation you came across, if every time fear started, if every time you argued, got angry or frustrated you opened yourself up to different perspectives and gave yourself more options....... How different would your life be?

Would this transform your life going forwards? Well, more options and more choices always gives us the chance to transform anything!

Always Seek Three Perspectives (and more if you can!)

EVOLUTION POINT NUMBER THIRTY-ONE

Change Your Incantations

"You talk to yourself, admit it, accept it and choose to be polite"

- *Graham Nicholls*

C hange Your Incantations

You know that you talk to yourself right? Of course you do, in fact you answered that question didn't you? (and that one!). We talk to ourselves every day and nearly every minute of every day, asking questions, making statements, creating meanings and deciding what to have to drink.

Have you noticed yourself repeating the same things, saying the same phrases to yourself time after time? These are what are known as incantations and they are extremely powerful in your life. So powerful, in fact, that changing them can create a huge shift, a true transformation in your life.

Consider for a moment, if you will, one of those phrases, sentences or questions that you repeatedly say to yourself. Think about it now, you know the one....... What is the exact wording you use? When do you use it? Does it crop up when good things happen or bad things? Do you use it in positive or negative times? If you can, write down the exact wording now and be specific (if you have more than one, and you may do, pick the one you think comes up the most).

When we repeatedly say the same things to ourselves we create a self fulfilling prophecy of who we are and what we want to happen. With each word we say to ourselves we effectively give both our conscious and unconscious mind commands, much like typing something into a computer and storing it in the hard drive. Our minds then respond to this, assuming it's the way we want to live our lives which creates the circle. The only question that remains........ Is the circle a positive, reinforcing one or a negative, disempowering circle?

There are two ways to look at the word "incantation"

In - CANT - ation

Or

In - CAN - tation

You are either telling yourself and your mind what you CAN do or what you CAN'T do with those repeated phrases. The more we repeat these incantations, the more we create the certainty that they are true and therefore we believe them from the deepest level. Which do you do at the moment, tell yourself you CAN do something or tell yourself you CAN'T do it?

Let's look at the example of a young man who once went to a Coach and said that he was having trouble with his career. He desperately wanted to move up the ladder of success, to be promoted in the company he worked for and yet it kept alluding him. His Coach started to dig deeper, asking questions about the young man, what he did when opportunities arose, what he thought and how he acted.

After a while the Coach had written a phrase down in his notes that the young man had repeated a few times so he decided to ask him about it. It turns out that the young man knew that he was saying this phrase to himself but never gave it any thought, it was just something he said. Yet right there, sat with his Coach repeating that phrase to him out loud it sounded horrible.... Was he really talking to himself in that way?

The Coach and the young man worked on slight changes to the phrase he was using so that the language would move in the right direction. The Coach knew that if he just changed it straight away it would probably be rejected so the alterations needed to be soft and staged. As they worked over the following weeks the young man started to catching himself starting to say the old phrase and quickly change it to the new ones they decided on. The more he caught himself and changed the phrase the quicker the old one lessened in its power and the new one grew in strength and when the next opportunity came up at work he was ready to pounce. Instead of holding himself back he was ready to apply for the new position and go after it with everything he had....... And as he walked into the interview he was repeating that new empowering phrase!

What was the negative in-CANT-ation the young man was using?

"I'm not sure I'm good enough to do that particular job"

It didn't matter if he was good enough, knew enough and had all the qualifications he needed. That one phrase stopped him from even applying for new positions, he had stopped himself before he had even started.

When changing these incantations we always start softly, remembering that we have been saying these things to ourselves and embedding them in our minds for years. To just directly change them will probably see them rejected out of hand and our attempts to replace the old with new will be fought against. However, if we start softly and build up to a more powerful incantation our chance of success increases tenfold.

Shall we carry on with the example from above? Remember that the negative in-CANT-ation was:

"I'm not sure I'm good enough to do that particular job"

A soft starting phrase to work around this might be something along the lines of:

"I'm starting to think I could do this"

The next step might be:

"I'm starting to believe I am good enough to do this job"

We then may follow up with:

"I think I've got what I need to take this job on"

And then the final shift to:

"I'm good enough to do what I choose to"

Each and every time that the old phrase rears its ugly head we follow the same pattern to start the replacement process, that pattern is:

- Recognise the old phrase
- Say 'No' to ourselves to disregard that phrase
- Say the new phrase to ourselves
- Repeat the new phrase 5 times

What does this do? It gives both our conscious and unconscious mind clear instructions. The "No" instructs that we do not want to think that way and the repeating of the new phrase says that this is how we are now choosing to think and believe.

How wide is the difference between:

"I'm not sure I'm good enough to do that particular job"

And

"I'm good enough to do what I choose to"

It's a HUGE difference isn't it? Take a look back at your main in-cantation, you know, the one I asked you to write down. Is it an in-CANT-ation or and in-CAN-tation? If it is on the negative, dis-empowering side are you ready to change it? It will take effort and it will transform your life.

Consider that phrase now and decide what a soft shift would be. Use the examples above if you wish and come up with a soft change. Using the word 'starting' is always a great soft shift...... "I'm starting to think" or "I'm starting to believe". Create three phrases that go from a soft shift right through to the opposite of your in-CANT-ation and write them all down.

You now have written down the old in-CANT-ation and your

shift phrases towards the in-CAN-tation. Start to recognise the old one every time you say it and follow the process above, using the first soft phrase for around 7 to 10 days and then moving to the next. The quicker and more often you catch the old phrase and change it, the more of its power you remove.

Will that phrase show up again even when you have shifted to the new one? Yes, it might, as it has been with you for a long time. Each time it does, follow the process and kill its power.

We use incantations every day of our lives, choosing which we will use is something that creates power within us....... Leaving the old ones alone removes our power.

The choice is yours!

Change Your Incantations!

EVOLUTION POINT
NUMBER THIRTY-TWO

Start Journaling

"A personal journal is an ideal environment in which to 'become'. It is a perfect place for you to think, feel, discover, expand, remember and dream"

\-   *Brad Wilcox*

Start Journaling

S It never ceases to amaze me just how much writing something down can open up your soul. Open you up to getting stuff out of you to resolve and also open you up to new ideas and experiences. The physical act of writing with pen and paper, while somewhat of a lost art these days it seems, has a magical quality to it. All your troubles can flow out of you in that moment while possibilities flow inwards.

I always encourage my clients to start journaling as they go through the Coaching journey with me. It helps them to process what we are going through within the sessions and also what they are going through in between sessions while life continues. It may seem a little old fashioned these days, with phones, tablets and laptops all able to be written on / in but there is something raw and emotional about writing with a pen on a clean piece of paper and my clients always report their experiences back to me as positive.

"When you write it, you invite it and when you read it, you feed it" - Graham Nicholls

What do you write in a journal though? Do you just pour your heart and soul into it whether they be good thoughts or bad? Do you write your wishes, dreams and goals?

Let me tell you what I write in my journal so that it may help you to decide what to write in yours. You don't have to follow my exact examples, they are here merely as thoughts and ideas. Your journal should always be about you and what you want to write.

The Day Just Past
I always write my journal at night, it sits on my nightstand, with its trusty pen for companion, waiting for me to climb into bed and let loose on its pages. I start with a quick description of what has happened in the last twenty-four hours, the good, the bad and the ugly. Just an overview and how I thought and reacted to each situation so that I can understand where I might want to improve should it arise again.

My Gratitude
Second I comment on what I am grateful for, both the things I

am grateful for in the day just past and also those things I am grateful for in life as a whole. I always write my top three to five things down and then add at least two new things each day. Reminding myself what I have to be grateful for each day gives me a moment to say thank you and ensures peaceful sleep.

A Goal Reminder
Every so often, usually 6 monthly, I write down the goals and targets that I want to achieve. I believe that when you write it down you invite it into your life and when you read it you feed the motivation and desire to go get it. Each day I will reflect on what I have done to move towards my goals and targets to remind me of them and how far I am along the path. Writing and reading goals is a massive part of the journey to achieving them.

Sign Off
Finally I sign off for the night with a simple "Thank You, Graham" as if I were signing a letter. This reflects the fact that what I am writing is not just for me, it is a message to the Universe that I am grateful for another day and every opportunity to learn, grow, contribute and love that has come my way that day.

My journal is like a private conversation between myself and the Universe that just doesn't seem right to have via a screen and keyboard. The words come from my thoughts and they come from my heart and they somehow enter the substance of life when they come out onto that page.

Journaling helps us on our journey into ourselves, that place where only we can go and only we can be discovered.

Start Journaling!

EVOLUTION POINT NUMBER THIRTY-THREE

Deal With Your Past, Not Live With It

"The past is behind, learn from it. The future is ahead, prepare for it. The present is here, live it."

\-   *Thomas S. Monson*

Deal With Your Past, Not Live With it

Deal With Your Past, Not Live With it

Do you know someone who lives in the past? You know the person I'm talking about here, the one that is always referring to the past as examples of either how good or bad it was. Have you ever noticed how skewed their recollection of it is whether focussing on either positive or negative?

We all create stories in our minds that define our experiences, these stories are our perspectives on the life we have led to this point. As we know from a previous chapter, however, is that our perspectives are different from anyone else's. The stories we create are ours and ours alone.

The problem is that when people consistently live in those stories their focus of the present reflects the past. These stories are created in three ways and in NLP (Neuro-Linguistic Programming) we call them "Generalisations', 'Distortions' and 'Deletions'.

Generalisation.

Someone who employs a Generalisation will create a view across a wide range of experiences or people based on their own history. For example; A woman who has been cheated on by her husband and hurt deep down emotionally might create the generalisation that all men are (insert your own expletive)! Or someone who has been mugged and stolen from could form the generalisation that going outside is dangerous and therefore they shut themselves away from the world.

This creates problems throughout their lives as it stops them from seeing the truth about any situation they come across. The woman who doesn't trust any men might meet the man of her dreams who would treat her properly, love and respect her. With her current generalisation though, she would dismiss him and never know the joy of that loving relationship.

The person who shuts themselves away from the world doesn't have the joy of ever walking in nature again, going to a party or even just having a coffee and chat with a friend. In both of these cases their lives are severely restricted and a breakthrough of the generalisation by seeking the truth would transform their lives. I'm not for one moment saying that the events that led to their situations were not hurtful and traumatic, what I am saying though is that they have a choice to react differently. Distortion.

Within any story there can be distortions of the truth, the parts where we can't remember quite what happened so our minds fill in the blanks. Have you ever played the game Chinese Whispers? Someone starts off by whispering something into someone's ear and they go and whisper what they think they heard into someone else's and so on. When you get to the tenth person, as an example, they say out loud what they think the original message was and it is often completely different to what was originally conveyed.

This is the brain at work, it hears part of the message and then creates the rest that it didn't hear. From a simple message you get a garbled version that bears no resemblance to the truth. Let's look at another example:

A couple have an argument that boils over and the sparks start to fly. One of them says something the other doesn't like so there's retaliation until eventually they are absolutely fuming with each other. They go off to do separate things, both still bubbling with angst and reliving the argument in their head. The only problem is, within their moments of anger they can't remember exactly what was said so they distort the truth making up parts of the conversation.

When they are both together again they decide to talk about it and sort it out. The only problem is that they now have very different versions of events as they have both distorted the conversation. There is huge potential for this to create another argument, or worse a separation with bad blood between the two forever more. Does this affect their future lives? If they continue to hold on to it then it most certainly will.

Deletion.

The mind also has the capacity to delete the things that are not important to us in a specific moment. Do you remember the exercise I asked you to do where you stopped for a moment and felt your pulse somewhere in your body? Is that always there? Yes, of course it is as your heart is still beating. The reason you don't feel it all the time is that the brain deletes it as unimportant. Much like it is deleting the feeling of your big toe on your right foot rubbing against your sock or shoe right now. The sensation was always there, it just wasn't important.

How does this affect our current lives? Let's visit another example:

Imagine a couple falling deeply in love and marrying knowing that they want to spend the rest of their lives together. They start to enjoy life and put everything into each others only for one of them to fall ill. They fight a long, painful battle with the illness while the other cares and tends to them but is helpless to do anything about the illness.

Eventually the person who fell ill passes away and the one left behind falls into a deep depression. The initial grief is devastating to them as they miss their life partner and the love they shared. However, as time goes on that grief turns to a deeper depression than before as they consistently remember the illness and suffering that their partner went through. They remember how helpless they felt despite their best efforts to keep the other comfortable. They remember the pain the sleepless nights.

Their memories of all the loving and joyful times are, at that moment, deleted from existence. As far as they are concerned they never happened, their whole life has become a long story of grief and sorrow. Of course, those memories are still there, just like your heart keeps beating and your pulse can still be felt when you focus on it. But for now they are gone and they live their lives that way.

"The past is gone, the future is yet to happen. Right now is the gift that it is why it is called the present"

We can only ever live in the here and now as this is the only moment we have. We can do nothing about the past as it has been and gone, there is no time travel and there is no changing the events. Those events from the past do not have a bearing on your life today unless you allow them to and that is your choice.

The way to let go of the past is a process of truth and gratitude. Searching for the truth in any situation and not getting caught up in the generalisation, distortions and deletions helps to work the past away. When we open up to the truth we start to accept that the past is gone and no matter what has happened we can only work with what we have right now.

Gratitude is essential to any life that wants to be more than what it currently is. It is only when we are grateful for what we have experienced and what we currently have that we can let go any move forward. Gratitude and giving thanks shuts the doors of anger, frustration, anxiety, depression and stress in the mind. It opens the doors of love and acceptance so that we can walk through them.

The past does not equal the future and it does not control the present, that responsibility resides solely on your shoulders.

Deal With Your Past, Not Live With It!

EVOLUTION POINT NUMBER THIRTY-FOUR

Be Perfect in Your Imperfections

"You are imperfect, you are wired for struggle, but you are worthy of love and belonging. Imperfections are not inadequacies; they are reminders that we are all in this together."

-   *Brene Brown*

Be Perfect in Your Imperfections

Be Perfect in Your Imperfections
Machines, designed by man, can make things as close to perfection as you can get…. Until the next machine comes along and makes it more perfectly. Yet we are not made by machines, we are creations of other human beings and of the

Universe (or another universal higher power of your choosing) in which we live. We were never born to be perfect and yet so many strive for it in all areas of their lives only to be denied it because of its very impossibility.

Whether it be striving for the perfect body through hours of training, or perfection of face through operations and money. It could be perfection of business or career through hours and hours of relentless work or striving for your idea of the perfect life.

There is a universal truth at play here, however, and that is the truth of balance. Everything the Universe offers requires balance and when we focus on one area in futile attempts to make it perfect there is another area that is faltering. The man who works tirelessly for hours on end to perfect his career yet his marriage fails. The woman who wants the perfect marriage and children yet is deeply unhappy due to the lack of living her true self as an artist or dancer...... these are obviously only examples.

"So should we just accept life where we are and say to hell with it Graham?" I hear you cry. Of course not. Another Universal truth is 'that which does not grow eventually dies" and it is hardwired into every living thing. We need to grow every single day to be happy and fulfilled but growth will never equal perfection for it is an endless journey of discovery. The only moment you stop growing is when you are at an end, *The* end.

Yet seeking perfection is not growth, in fact I'd offer the thought that it is just the opposite. When you seek perfection you trap every other part of you in a cage and a small cage at that. Did you know that if you put a baby shark in a small tank it will only grow to a size that is suitable to that tank but if you put it in the ocean it will grow to it's natural size.

Seeking perfection puts you in a tank and stunts your growth!

Why is perfection unattainable? Imagine if we were all perfect..... We would all be the same and life would be very boring. Our imperfections make us unique and individual, they attract us to each other and they are to be celebrated in their perfection.

If I were the same as you there would be no point in me writing this book nor you reading it. We would have the same knowledge and experience making all books irrelevant, all knowledge irrelevant...... life irrelevant.

But it is more than that, people wait for the perfect timing or until a project is finished and perfect before releasing it. They then struggle to find the perfect time as timing isn't perfect and, indeed, time itself is a construct of our consciousness if you remember that discussion point from earlier in the book.

If I were to wait until this book was perfect I would never release it as I could read it through a hundred times and make changes to different parts each time. It would be a different day with different experiences and I might be thinking differently. I put across my points as best I can in any given moment and allow them to flow through me as the Universe sees fit.

You are already perfect in your imperfections, you are enough, good enough and worthy of everything the Universe has to offer........ You just need to know it in your heart.

Grow daily..... Yes!

Be Perfect in Your Imperfections..... Absolutely!

EVOLUTION POINT NUMBER THIRTY-FIVE

Let Go and Let Grow

"In the process of letting go, you will lose many things from the past, but you will find yourself"

\-   *Deepak Chopra*

L et Go and Let Grow

Have you noticed how so many people are on a mission these days, they are on a mission to achieve everything and control their entire world. If it can be measured they measure it, if it can't be measured they want to find a way to measure it. We talked about instant gratification earlier in the book and that too is a symptom of wanting to control anything and everything.

We all know that control is a fallacy though right? We can never control something as free flowing as the energy the Universe provides nor the energy that flys around inside us like hyper-speed train on overload.

Joy and love in life come to us when we let go, when we accept who we are and where we are and that the Universe will show us the way. It's somewhat of a new way of thinking, particularly for me as a Coach. Coaching is about setting goals and targets, finding the actions that will take us to that goal, drumming up motivation and desire to take the actions and following through. What if there was another way?

What if we were to decide on the purpose of our being and then let go? What if we were to believe that the Universe would show us how to get there when we ask the question of it? The Universe is constantly throwing stuff our way to help us live the life we want when we are authentic with who we are. When we get in tune with the vibrations, with our path in the Universe then how we are to get where we want to go lights up like a runway in front of us.

You'll remember, I'm certain, me saying that there is a universal law that states that which does not grow will eventually die. Well the Universe doesn't want you to die until it's your time (and then it's your body and not your spirit). What the Universe really wants is for you to continue growing so it will provide that growth for you in any form possible. When you let go and have faith in the fact that the Universe will take care of it for you..... It does.

Growth becomes a given, an enjoyable process of daily learnings that lead you along the path to who and what you want to be. A path that leads to you ultimately fulfilling your purpose, that which you were put here for. As a creation of the Universe it knew what your purpose was long before you were born but we, as Human Beings, try to take over. We think we know better, we think we can control every aspect of our lives and then wonder why things don't work out. Things only work out when we let the Universe work it out for us.

Stop expecting everything to be right, it won't be..... That's not how life works. Stop believing you can control life circumstances...... life will prove you wrong. Accept that the path is already laid out for you and is well lit for your journey and have faith that your path will find you and not the other way around.

If you want to wrap all of this up in one word, that word would be *acceptance*. Acceptance of who you are and where you are and that the Universe has your back. Not that you shouldn't work and take actions towards where you want to be, acceptance is more about not being frustrated and upset with where you currently are. Those emotions simply take away your energy and move you out of your vibration with the Universe. Acceptance keeps you in that flow of vibration and allows you to see the path lit before you.

Letting go requires faith and belief, these both stem from one place.... The heart. It is your heart that accepts, it is your heart that forgives, it is your heart that develops faith and has true belief. Let your heart be at peace and life will find you.

Let Go and Let Grow!

EVOLUTION POINT NUMBER THIRTY-SIX

Drop Your Ego, Resonate Abundance

"The Ego is not who you really are. The ego is your self-image; it is your social mask; it is the role you are playing. It thrives on approval, it wants control and it is sustained by power...... because it lives in fear"

- *Deepak Chopra*

D rop Your Ego, Resonate Abundance

STOP! Before you go running off just because the word 'abundance' has come up.

Some of you reading this will have been slightly turned off by that word because for so many it resonates negative connotations of money. People who speak about having abundance can often be seen as the ones who are creating their own abundance by taking your money.

If you have that belief, I completely respect it because I used to have that belief as well. It wasn't until I discovered the truth that I was able to let all of that stuff go and realise what true abundance really is. But more of that in a few moments, let's talk EGO to start with.

It is the ego that thinks abundance is about money and things, the ego wants to own, control and thinks mine.... Mine..... MINE. Have you seen the film "Finding Nemo"? In it there is a scene where there are loads of Seagulls on a dock and when a fish jumps up in the air they all start shouting "mine, mine, mine, mine, mine" - this is what I see, hear and feel as the ego.

The ego is what tells you that you have to have more stuff, the thing that wants you to keep up with your family, friends and even the neighbours. The ego also gets you to put on a false personality in front of other people and that false personality becomes a cage that traps you every time you see them.... And then traps you for life. As far as I can tell, there is no positive side to the ego and the sooner we drop it from our lives, the sooner our lives will transform.

Dropping your ego takes work, I'm here to tell you the truth and that's the truth right there. You see, there's every chance your ego has had some form of control over you for many years because, as with so much of this important information, we are not taught this at school. In fact, at school is where the ego starts its developmental journey. As we start to figure out who we are and our own internal conversation kicks into gear we want to find our tribe, we want to fit in. Very often though, to fit in, we feel like we have to become someone else and that, right there, is the start of the ego.

If you have, or have had, teenage children you'll know exactly what I'm talking about. That moment when they come home and they are not talking like your child anymore is a moment that takes most parents by surprise. All of a sudden you seem to have someone else's child on your hands, it may look like your child but it no longer sounds like them. They are using words and phrases that you would have never associated with them before, they go from playing with toys to wanting stuff..... Mobile phones, different clothes.... They want their stuff and they want to do what they want when they want to do it.

You may say that this is just them discovering themselves but I would disagree..... It is them discovering their ego. Is it an important part of their development, yes. Is it up to us as parents to teach them about ego and the negative impact it will have on their lives? Heck yes because school never will.

But what of you and I? How do we let go of our ego? This is where the truth about abundance comes into play!

Abundance is a way of living that allows us to see the true beauty of life itself. For when we resonate with true abundance our eyes open and see past physical possessions and the things we want. Resonating with abundance allows love, joy, excitement and fulfilment into our life... for that is surely what an abundant life is! Smelling the beautiful rose, tasting the fresh water, feeling how much you are loved, hearing the bird song and seeing the beauty of the world around you is the realm of abundance.

The ego does not care for such things and, as such, is undone by abundance for Love, Joy and Fulfilment and will always overcome physical gains. Abundance, therefore, is the antidote to the ego and yet so many see scarcity where abundance is so..... Well..... Abundant.

While you believe in scarcity that is exactly what will persist in your life for we create that which we focus on. When we focus on the lack of joy in our lives, joy will never be able to find us. When we focus on the scarcity of love or happiness these too will escape our grasp. Making the shift to understanding and believing that the Universe supplies everything in abundance will create a shift towards those things being attracted to you.

Imagine Abundance and Scarcity being two sides of a magnet; when the scarcity sides are facing each other they force each other apart no matter how hard you try to push them together. When the abundance sides are facing each other they snap together and stay stuck in place, they attract each other without thought or desire. This is the power of abundance, the power that the Universe provides.

When you shift to believing in the power of abundance you step into the vibration of the Universe and the ego is destroyed. Love, joy, fulfilment flow to you naturally and stay in your life as you self fulfil your own prophecy of abundance. You are, after all, your own self fulfilling prophecy throughout your life aren't you? If you focus on scarcity it is scarcity that will prevail. When you focus on abundance then your life will be filled and fulfilled. It's you choice.

"Wait a minute Graham, what if I do want money? After all I need money to live right!"

Let me make this clear, I used the example of money at the start of this section because so many people have that negative connotation to abundance and money. The truth is that there is an abundance of anything we want but while we continue to see that negative connotation we continue to see scarcity. What does scarcity bring? You got it..... Scarcity.

Drop the ego and create an abundant life of love, joy and fulfilment first and you will see its power and you can then start to believe in the abundance of all things. Dr Wayne Dyer used to say that an abundance of anything in life was like the ocean, you can take a cup full from it or you can fill a tanker from it and the drop in the level is so tiny it cannot be measured.

The ego does not serve you, it serves itself. Abundance does not serve itself, it offers itself to you.

Drop Your Ego, Resonate Abundance!

EVOLUTION POINT NUMBER THIRTY-SEVEN

You Come From Greatness

"Most people think that they are humans having a spiritual experience. I prefer to see myself as a spiritual being having a temporary human experience"

-   *Dr Wayne Dyer*

You Come From Greatness

You Come From Greatness
So we come to the final section of this book. Thank you for getting here, so many will not have followed through having been caught up in fear or defiant in their own thinking. That's not to say that I believe I am correct in everything I have

said, I am always open to new ways of thinking and being. In fact, the truth of it is that I'm not sure I wrote this book! The words simply came through me so that you could read them and take from them what you wish.

Right there, in that sentence is what this book is really about, the fact that this is not about me nor you. It is about something that we are a much bigger part of; the greatness of this amazing life, this incredible planet and this wonderful Universe. No matter what your beliefs, whether they be in a religious figure, the Universe, a Source of Being or anything else, there is one thing that holds true.

You come from greatness!

You are part of the plan, you are part of the creative make up of this world and the universe and your energy, soul and spirit are part and parcel in the very fabric of it all. Each of us was selected to be born, one chance in millions, if not billions, that it would be us. Everything in the entire universe had to come together at just the right moment for us to have been created and yet here we are, a part of this wonderful thing we call life.

If you didn't have your part to play you simply wouldn't have been here, you wouldn't have made it past all of those challenges. And yet you are here, you jumped the hurdles, crossed the rivers, broke through the walls and here you sit ready to play your part..... But what is that part?

I hope, in some way, this book will have given you some insights which will allow you to answer that. The answers were never meant to come to us easily, that is part of the journey we must go on to transform our lives and it's a journey that never ends. It is a journey though, that was only meant for the selected few and you were given life to be one of those few.

Not only do you come from greatness, your are greatness!

The world and the universe are better places for your being a part of them. You are needed, required, wanted, loved, enough and worthy of your part..... If you weren't, you would not be here.

You do not just come from greatness...... You Are Greatness.

A FEW FINAL THOUGHTS

There we have it, my friend, I hope you don't mind me calling you a friend? It feels like we've been a journey together even though we may have never met. I would like you to read that final paragraph again for it is the one truth I hold.......

The world and the universe are better places for your being a part of them. You are needed, required, wanted, loved, enough and worthy of your part..... If you weren't, you would not be here.

Any and all of the sections of this book can help you to transform your life and yet you need but one to have the life you want, your belief in those words above. If, at the moment, you are not quite sure don't worry. It is quite normal as we have been filled with the opposite information for most of our lives and it takes time to make such a shift.

Over the next few days and weeks just allow the thought to work its way into you and allow yourself to be handed over to the thought that you are enough and you are worthy. Open up your heart and soul and it will tell you the truth, allowing that truth to reach out to every part of you. As this happens, life transforms almost effortlessly (you need to do your part of course) and becomes that which you were put here for.

I wish you well my friend on your journey through life. Whether we meet one day or whether we remain friends in this book,

I know you are here for a reason and that reason is yours and yours alone.

My Best Regards
Graham

P.S.

If you would like a few extra resources for your learning journey, why not check out some of my online courses. Here's a link so that you can see what is on offer:

www.thepriorityacademy.com/courses

THE END

"When you see every beginning as an end and every end as a beginning life suddenly has a beautiful flow to it"

- Graham Nicholls

Made in United States
North Haven, CT
08 March 2022

16903667R00098